# Spectral Realms

No. 20 ‡ Winter 2024

Edited by S. T. Joshi

The spectral realms that thou canst see
With eyes veil'd from the world and me.

H. P. LOVECRAFT, "To a Dreamer"

SPECTRAL REALMS is published twice a year by Hippocampus Press,
P.O. Box 641, New York, NY 10156 (www.hippocampuspress.com).
Copyright © 2024 by Hippocampus Press.
All works are copyright © 2024 by their respective authors.
Cover art by Pinckney Marcius-Simons,
*La Vision du Demon* (*Vision of a Demon*), c. 1900.
Cover design by Daniel V. Sauer.
Hippocampus Press logo by Anastasia Damianakos.

ISBN 978-1-61498-423-8          ISSN 2333-4215

# Contents

**Poems** .................................................................................. 5

   Memento Mori / John Shirley ........................................................ 7
   Into the Mouth of the Sea / Maxwell I. Gold ................................. 8
   For an Autumn Willow / Scott J. Couturier ................................... 9
   The Baker at the Beggar's Wedding / Amelia Gorman ................. 10
   The Tryst / Frank Coffman ........................................................... 13
   Salute to Robert E. Howard: A Texas Writer / Carl E. Reed ......... 14
   Miranda's Resolve / Kyla Lee Ward ............................................. 15
   dark wishes / Lee Clark Zumpe ................................................... 16
   A Casting Out: A Failure / Benjamin Blake ................................. 17
   Dark Axiom / Manuel Pérez-Campos .......................................... 18
   Mother of Our Fate / DJ Tyrer ..................................................... 20
   A Hollow Heart / Deborah L. Davitt ........................................... 22
   The Bone Man / Joshua Green ..................................................... 23
   Necropolis / Kurt Newton ............................................................ 24
   Lord and Lady / Andrew White .................................................. 25
   The Moon Is Made of Cat / Katherine Kerestman ....................... 26
   The March / Ngo Binh Anh Khoa ................................................ 27
   Verses inspired by *Le Horla* / Scott J. Couturier ......................... 28
   Shoggoths / Leigh Blackmore ...................................................... 31
   Some Books Are Forbidden for Good Reason / Darrell Schweitzer ..... 32
   Primal Night / Ann K. Schwader .................................................. 33
   Night of the Dove / David Barker ................................................ 34
   Tatterjack; or, The Murder of Mother Goose /
      Adam Bolivar and Steven Withrow ....................................... 35
   Gaia's Prophecy / John Shirley ..................................................... 43
   Echoing Dylan Thomas; or, A Cri de Coeur from Reader to
      Writer / Carl E. Reed ............................................................. 46
   That Was Epic / Maxwell I. Gold ................................................. 48
   Reading by Ghost Light / Dmitri Akers ....................................... 49
   How Love Fled / Simon MacCulloch ........................................... 50
   Moonfog / Wade German ............................................................ 51
   Anathema / Lori R. Lopez ............................................................ 52
   The Gorgon Queen / Ron L. Johnson II ...................................... 56

The Savage Fantasies of Mr. Arbuthnot / Manuel Pérez-Campos ......57
After Heathcliff Digs Up Cathy / Michael Potts ......58
The Doom / Geoffrey Reiter ......59
The Monsters of the Moor / Frank Coffman ......60
In Lakewood Cemetery / Tylor James ......64
Sacred / Lee Clark Zumpe ......67
vampire dragon: a haiku / Kendall Evans ......68
The Great and Final Feast / Jay Sturner ......69
Lunar Mission / Katherine Kerestman ......71
Beneath the Mirror Moon / Ngo Binh Anh Khoa ......72
The Torment of Flame / Deborah L. Davitt ......73
Love Came upon a Darkling Night / William Clunie ......74
Hic Aqua Est / Joshua Gage ......78
Malvolio's Revenge / Kyla Lee Ward ......79
By Creator Forsaken / Scott J. Couturier ......80
Grave-Robbing 2.0: Intermediate / Darrell Schweitzer ......82
A Vision of Carcosa / David C. Kopaska-Merkel ......84
The Night of Mirth and Magic / Andrew White ......85
There upon the Threshold / Carl E. Reed ......86
Telos Falling / Maxwell I. Gold ......87
Daughters of Phorcys / Wade German ......88
Ravensong / Lori R. Lopez ......93
Of Shapeshifters Spawned by the Revolution / Manuel Pérez-Campos ... 94
Sea Dream / Simon MacCulloch ......96
Dark Sister / Lee Clark Zumpe ......97
Infernal Nocturne / Ngo Binh Anh Khoa ......98
The Skeleton Dance / Joshua Green ......101

**Classic Reprints** ......103
A Dream / William Sharp ......105
Fog / Mary C. Shaw ......106

**Reviews** ......107
Mythology and Cosmicism / S. T. Joshi ......109

**Notes on Contributors** ......111

**Index to *Spectral Realms* 11–20** ......119

Poems

# Memento Mori

*John Shirley*

His eyes are white-light ceiling bulbs; his teeth syringe needles—
he's attended by a retinue of shiny scarab beetles.
I stood a-teetering on the vacuum-breathing brink,
where you fall with the weight of a single thought you think;
where laughing things rise to find they truly sink
and white on white on white on white—is the color of my ink.
I didn't pass through the tunnel, the tunnel passed through me
And death will not hesitate, to come unseasonably

*Memento mori*, I remember death—I recall it clearly, yes yes yes:
I've bargained with that smug old merchant of rest;
though that time is past, and I pretend we never met
you know what hasn't happened—will, onward, happen yet.

I no longer taunt the lion, nor will I walk the edge;
I withdrew from the void that shimmers past the ledge.
But every morning when I wake, I see the shadows smile;
I know that it is but his whim to smirk and bide a while.

# Into the Mouth of the Sea

## Maxwell I. Gold

There, atop the highest crooked obelisk in a nameless city, trapped in some moist dark chamber, I watched the oceans reclaim the world with ruinous persistence. Below, the waters thrashed with a raucous envy as they sought to pull the basalt and marble tower tumbling down toward the crushing, stupendous depths. Within the tower, concrete, chain, and metal bent acrimoniously, unwilling to give up beneath the tremendous pain; bits and bark-like crumbs smashing around my feet where the waters howled into the night, their deep songs of rage bellowed heavy against the stars themselves.

There had to be a way out, oxygen became as scarce as diamonds, and the laughter of the seas mixed in the bitter stink of death, drowned the pleas of a billion lights in a storm of indifference.

*Not like this.*

Utterly helpless, the tower swayed unceasingly in the gray, spectral skies ready to fall into the whirling jaws of the wild seas. The music of the ocean became more dissonant, below, above, and all around pronounced with a sinister reclamation as the waves grew even deadlier, cold like steel daggers shattered the glass windows cutting me down a piece by piece—blood and salt—swallowed entirely by the mouth of the seas.

*Dear god,*
   *not like this.*

# For an Autumn Willow

*Scott J. Couturier*

Willow gilt with Autumn's gold:
Forlorn gusts your bowers sway,
Last sun's light a fading gray
On leaves which, weeping, unfold.

Willow with Fall's favor crowned:
Drowse at close of dreary day.
Crows about your arbors play,
Woodlands around in fire gowned.

Willow spread with yellow shawl:
Nothing can make Summer stay,
May a good sixmonth away.
Sorrowful you shed your pall.

Willow charged by season's change:
Boughs ablaze in sunset's ray,
Burning now with colors fey.
Twilight falls, makes all things strange:
Wonder by Nature arranged.

Willow with your beauty bowed:
Moonrise in starry array
Limns in argent your display.
Auric-laureled, you bend proud.

# The Baker at the Beggar's Wedding

*Amelia Gorman*

Me, I baked the same cakes every week
honey and saffron, lemon rind
topped with roses and scattered silver dragees,
layered with violets smashed with sugar and wine.

My bakery at heart was a modest affair
serving tired sweets to tired people
for tired marks in Marburg town where
nothing ever changed for me.

Until *he* came in, mite-riddled mantel of fox skin,
trousers half lichen, dropped a pile of coins from China,
other coins with Nero's head, coins from Minos, Devon's tin,
said when he returned I should give him something wild.

So I stacked together a tower of almond,
silver and pumpkin, cashew and lime
orgeat leaking out the sides, and
spun around with honeysuckle vine.

He came back to collect as the sun started to rise
his glare was as red and cracked as my own.
Terrifying skyflowers burned in his eyes
when he cast that fire down on my labor.

"You passed, this shows promise," with needles
in his voice after licking the edge and taking a bite.
"Now tonight bring one even stranger where the beetles
burrow under the tallest pine, in the cold moonlight."

I fattened the crumb with grease of goose
and all day I worked with loam and thyme.
I brought it to the woods under the full moon
with the sweetness of beach apple, bitter quinine.

Women were dancing with men and with beasts,
the beggar's bride wore a dress of spun amber.
Serpents and weasels wound round the feasts
that were laid out at the beggar's wedding.

When it came time for me to serve, I cut with grace
into the rich moist soil, dripping with pride.
The groom, still in tatters, dove in for a taste
and said, "Do it again tomorrow for my second bride."

I went further, I baked with ergot mold,
rainwater, amanita, and the morning's rime,
maple syrup spun into threads of gold,
and emeralds of the finest grind

And the women tore off their clothes, perchance
they were more than clothes. A hedgehog beat the time
on primeval drums, a swarm of lice asked me to dance
and I accepted, while the bride walked down the aisle.

The second bride threw off her wedding veil
and the groom tore off his pants
he had been hiding hooves, and a hairy tail,
and I didn't remember anything after that.

Next I baked with rotten bluebells
and a kid's blood, antique silver chimes.
I borrowed a bone saw from the barber next door . . .
I held a bolt cutter to my tongue before . . .
I took from the back of a cupboard my marrow spoon . . .
*and, for the third bride, baked in some things of mine.*

# The Tryst

*Frank Coffman*

> It was last Hallowe'en, the haunted, the dread,
>     In the wind-tattered wood, by the storm-twisted pine,
> That I, who am living, kept tryst with the dead,
>     And clasped her a moment who once had been mine.
>         —Madison Julius Cawein, "Halloween"

I come to keep my tryst with one now dead.
I walk the forest path where last we tread
Hand-in-hand beneath a lowering sky
(We could not know that she was soon to die),
But—this time—with a sense of awful dread.

I've found the spot appointed where she said
She loved me, and agreed that we should wed,
That this would be "our spot, our place" for aye.
I came to keep my tryst.

Wind whispers through the branches overhead,
And—on the wind—the voice of she now fled!
It brings a message I cannot deny.
Another must depart—and it is I!
Ah! She is here . . . with arms outspread!
And I shall keep my tryst.

# Salute to Robert E. Howard: A Texas Writer

*Carl E. Reed*

> "All fled—all done, so lift me on the pyre—
> The feast is over, and the lamps expire."
> —The last words Bob Howard left on his typewriter shortly before he killed himself, age 30.

He birthed the savage Hyborian Age:
brutal men of indomitable will
sprung with wild, fierce oaths from the crimson page—
Cimmerian battle cries echo still.
His evocative prose cut sharp as flint;
the grimdark poetry: haunting & stark.
He attacked the typewriter, eyes aglint;
"Two-Gun Bob" left his literary mark.
A bare-knuckle brawler too sensitive
to witness the death of his beloved dog;
his heroes were brooding, contemplative
their violent lives picaresque travelogues.
Howard's tales were e'en then out of fashion:
pulp eruptions of pulse-pounding passion.

# Miranda's Resolve

*Kyla Lee Ward*

Her coronet they seek, perhaps her life.
Milan is far too rich a prize to lie,
Within magician's daughter. Prince's wife
Cannot evade the inquisition's eye.
She never bound her friends as did her sire—
that airy sprite is yet among her spies.
The water nymphs assist with such enquire,
As may demand exchange of pearls for eyes.
A Caliban of clay she may compile,
To stalk and slay, and then again be still.
But Naples offers something that the isle
Could not supply, so there she bends her will.
From Vulcan she extracts a mighty boon:
If she should burn, the rest will follow soon.

# dark wishes

*Lee Clark Zumpe*

ancient stars sweep sickened skies
in an endless procession,
disbursing and realigning
in a somnolent ballet

too protracted to be observed,
too complex to be calculated
by all but the most fastidious
and dutiful disciple.

their wan light cast vast
aeons passed shines feebly
upon crumbling steeples and
narrow cobblestone alleys

over battlefields and burial grounds
and zealously guarded borders;
across bloated refugee camps
and into homeless shelters

and on sleepy towns
where chronic apathy,
misplaced prejudice and callousness
breed dark wishes.

# A Casting Out: A Failure

*Benjamin Blake*

The exorcism didn't work.
I still catch glimpses of its shadow
Flittering in the peripheral.
And at night
When I'm alone in my barely furnished room,
I can't sleep
For fear of its return.

The voices come unannounced,
A whisper, a scream inside the skull.
Spirits unable to be distilled,
Driving a man to drink
Until he falls into sweet oblivion.

I am sickened by what I have become,
And the jet-black creature
Which dwells deep inside,
Is melding with bones
That grow too weary
To offer any real resistance.

And in all likelihood
I will die
Before it does.
But what will become
Of the husk left behind?

# Dark Axiom

## *Manuel Pérez-Campos*

> . . . it is best not to exist at all.
> —H. P. Lovecraft, "Nietzscheism and Realism"

While chasing on Appaloosa and rifle
a great thunderbird of opal feathers
I, in questing headband and loincloth,
was drawn out of a nimbus-penumbraed
complex of knolls into a broad plain of
dust and salt by a dim stubborn glint near
its center which began to intensify and
greaten after I—as if to a forbidden privilege
or a long-delayed adventure—urged
my mount impulsively to full gallop.
I halted abruptly with half a league
to go, and after a short introspective
interval in which the only sound was
that of the wind causing the boulders
around us to vibrate thinly, resumed
my advance albeit at a much slackened
pace until positioned gently before
a prodigious alien ice crystal taller by far
than us both. Afflicted by recurrent
sheens of phantasmal green, its six

arms, raying out like frozen solar flares
and tapering to flame-pointed tips,
had already begun to curl steeply inward,
as though in liaison with those about
to shrivel radically and disappear. I sensed
it was a progeny of the humming
of the black abyss and that long ago
it had attained godhood, yet one
vulnerable to every travail imaginable, that
it might continue to extend its sublime
mental frontiers. Poised like a rigid
pharaoh from a land east of dreams
and west of reality as it dripped
dangerously under the swollen aura
of an inescapable red star, it relayed
telepathically that there was more
poignancy in the state of non-arising
than in a temporal manifestation such
as it or I: trying to overcome the folly I
was heir to, I tried to question it further,
but its silence went straight to the heart.

# Mother of Our Fate

*DJ Tyrer*

From the gaping void
The womb of Chaos
Darkness and Night come
Bearing their sister Earth
Swaddling Her comfortingly
Until their daughter
Day issued from Night's womb
Allowing Her mother a brief rest
From Her guardian duties
Caressing the Earth with Her light
Then Night returns
Taking Her sister Earth
Once more in her arms
Her children scattering forth
To supervise the world's primal needs
Aloof from the wars
Of Gods, Titans and Men
Safe in the care of their mother
Dispensing dreams and fate
Neither the raging storm
Nor the quaking ground
Not even the overseer of the dead
Can challenge Her or Her children
She is primal, eternal
Unending

Mother of our fate
No slings and arrows can defeat her
Even the Earth is in awe
The eldest, the greatest
Undefeated
Ultimately incomprehensible
Goddess of the Gods
Night

# A Hollow Heart

*Deborah L. Davitt*

I wish I could love you,
but my heart feels as empty
as an ossuary;

the dry, bone-filled chambers
of my soul rattle;
ribs clatter like wind-chimes.

The smooth, round caps
of skulls
make hollow, horrid drums;

teeth chatter here
like the sound
of endless words.

I wish I could love you
as you deserve to be,
but I'm empty,

and I am the grave
in which all my dreams
lie dead.

# The Bone Man

*Joshua Green*

Beneath the earth there lives a man of bones,
Decrepit with eyes wet like yawning caves,
He sits alone without a son and groans,
To all the dead that lay above in graves.
He came upon this place at twilight, for
The pond that drowned his son had then become
A thin-space to the Land of Death, a door
Begot by dying suns where all go numb.
He stepped into the changing pool, the shade
Of dusk now ever present, falling through
The earth into a gentle sea, to wade
And swim to an island of endless rue.
Here The Bone Man remains, a lonely husk,
Until another swims the pond at dusk.

# Necropolis

### *Kurt Newton*

We could have explored for days but we soon found our answer
At the far outer edges of the silent city sprawl:
What looked like another impressively engineered landscape
Was a burial ground created wholly from the bones of the dead.

It was here we discovered the sad truth of its creators:
They had waited out time until there was time no more,
Written in the glyphs of their arcane language
A eulogy of a culture forever lost to the world.

Our translators told a tale of desperate survival
When the surface of the planet became increasingly uninhabitable;
An impending doom of catastrophic proportions
Brought then down deep down into the folds of the Earth.

Waiting for millennia through one cataclysm after another,
Watching the rise and fall leave its mark on the cavern walls
While the graveyard grew like a great sequoian spirit forest
Until the last procession crossed the ultimate threshold.

# Lord and Lady

*Andrew White*

I am the son of morning
And the daughter of the night.
My heart hears a warning,
I'm blinded by light—
A thousand shades of white.

I am the prince of new life
And the duchess of decay.
Born again on the edge of a knife,
I start anew at the end of day—
Blackened skies will lead the way.

I am the lord of the summer
And the lady of wintertime.
I follow the distant drummer,
Crawling through filth and through grime—
Descending toward the sublime.

# The Moon Is Made of Cat

*Katherine Kerestman*

The moon is really a furball,
A gray-and-white mottled cat,
Guardian of the high heavens,
Curled up into a spiral,
White whiskers taken for moonbeams
From earthly low vantage point.
Tail curled up underneath her,
Sweeps worlds away when it bristles,
And arching her spine grinds up stars
To millions of crystalline shards.

# The March

*Ngo Binh Anh Khoa*

The crimson dust storm is our war-god's breath
That leads our march towards each ravaged field
Seized by the Dark Lord's beasts. We shall not yield
Till those fell fiends are offered up to Death.
Harken! The Heavens' war-drums thunder nigh;
Each lightning flash incites our warriors' screams
For blood, whose brilliance sharpens our blades' gleams,
Banishing the gathered shades that cloak the sky.
Forth! forth we march, and forth we charge—towards
The blasphemous hordes of imps and walking corpses,
And hosts of snake-men, trolls, and bat-winged horses—
To win back freedom with our righteous swords.
Forth! Brothers, sisters! raise your hallowed steel!
Have Evil witness Man's true might and kneel!

# Verses inspired by *Le Horla*
(for Guy de Maupassant)

*Scott J. Couturier*

There was no warning—
no siren announcing your arrival.
On a joyous, carefree spring day,
inspired by idle pleasure
I waved to a passing white-hulled ship.
Yet somehow, my actions summoned
you forth from that vessel,
where you preyed on sailor & passenger,
into my very home & hearth:
an invisible but tangible presence,
a Thing without perceivable form,
but *with form*,
for I see you obscure my reflection
in the antique mirror, I do!

Madness is another name for inevitability:
we are all made to pretend this world
is a good world, a sane world. You taught
me this day-by-day, as you drank water
& milk from sealed vessels, as you
intruded hourly upon my sovereign will.
Obsession drives me now,
to unmask what is unseen—
in my chambers by night, you

stir & brush against me, sending tender
feelers into my mind & peeling asunder
gray matter, transplanting your whims,
your desires, & at night I waken to you
sitting, gloating, on my chest!

Ah! Waking & sleeping alike a horror,
with you, *Horla*, imposing on my mind
& body, soul & psyche. Only one solution:
to burn, burn you alive, if you can be said to live,
& now, reports from Brazil tell of
more of your kind, unknown thousands more,
creating an epidemic of insanity!
Is it my mere madness which misinforms?
Or is this the nascent stage of an invasion,
your kind come to conquer mine,
Outsiders swarming from sidereal Space & Time
to overtake humanity's race, to enslave & devour
us, to wield us like tools, to feed on our life
& our terror, our humiliation at subjugation!

The fire is lit: I will burn you to unseen cinders,
sacrifice myself likewise before I allow you to take
my mind! *Horla*, odious & oppressive Other,
entity which wears insanity as disguise:

I watch blue flames flare up burgundy curtains,
coil & consume my bed where I have writhed
in torment beneath your ministrations.
With a laugh such as Lot may have given
when his wife crystallized to salt,
I flee that conflagration, only outside
hearing screaming from upstairs rooms,
servants roasting alive, unthought-of in my
momentary vengeful derangement,
my ritual of cleansing incineration.

# Shoggoths

*Leigh Blackmore*

Whence dreaded Ubbo-Sathla came, they come—
These protoplasmic beings of vast size;
The depths of earth's dim caverns they will plumb;
They probe the dark with glistening moist eyes

That form and re-form, myriads on their skins.
Self-luminous and shapeless, black as slime,
Their iridescent, evil, alien grins
Grow formless as they slither out of time.
These mutant congeries—like Elder Things—
Pustules in motion, trailing foetid strings!

# Some Books Are Forbidden for Good Reason

*Darrell Schweitzer*

Suppose I hold in my hands an infinite picture album,
in which you can never find the same page twice,
and each of the beautifully rendered, superbly detailed
scenes of strange cities or worlds,
or portraits, multifarious, enigmatic,
comes into existence when I turn over a leaf,
and vanishes into oblivion when I turn another.
Suppose, as I very much suspect, this is also true
of the subjects depicted, created and destroyed
like passing shadows, as the pages must inevitably be turned.
Have I become a god, a master of life and death
for countless millions?
I can't keep it open to a single page forever.
What if I find a portrait of myself in that book,
and in panic or just carelessness, snap it shut?

I wonder what became of the previous owner.

# Primal Night

*Ann K. Schwader*

So little still endures of primal night
that Earth has lost all sense of it. Nowhere
remains its realm: our oceans, land, & air
alike illuminated by the blight
of our incessant lives. We've crowded out
the dark that spawned our gods of storm & blood,
mythologies of famine & the Flood
all drowned alike in light. Cut free from doubt
but seeking space, we fix upon the moon's
deep polar craters rich with water ice,
& midnight yet indelible. To claim
the first awakes the second. All too soon,
our thirst is slaked . . . before we learn its price,
as grasping shadows whisper fear's lost name.

# Night of the Dove

*David Barker*

I find myself alone, the stars above
The only light to guide me through that maze
Of stony walls, above which flies the dove;
Somehow, I know she keeps me in her gaze.
As one, we pierce the city's sullen core.
A thousand fires now rage in nearby streets
And echoed screams of horror the crow repeats
Like necromancer's uttered outré lore.

Unholy swarms that dance to rhythmic drums
On all sides reach to grab me as I pass.
I sense this dove has flown through regions vast,
Transversing space where idiot Thog thrums.
When suddenly the squab shoots like a streak—
A detached finger carried in her beak!

Inspired by H. P. Lovecraft's sonnet "X. The Pigeon-Flyers" in *Fungi from Yuggoth*.

# Tatterjack; or, The Murder of Mother Goose
A Ballad

*Adam Bolivar and Steven Withrow*

I tell the tale of Tatterjack,
    A strange one to be sure;
He dressed in tatters, all in black,
    Outmoded his couture.

To Boston did that hob-thrall sail,
    Sent by the Queen of Fae;
To win release he could not fail
    Her enemy to slay:

Elizabeth, called Mother Goose,
    Who sung the faery verse
That if beyond the Isles was loose
    Would spell a heavy curse.

The Queen of Faerie's light would wane,
    Her glamour dimmed and weak,
Which on the earth would end her reign,
    Her fortunes turning bleak.

Gulls like buzzards overhead;
    Wharf rats showed their teeth
At the raggy heap of sack and thread
    And the human underneath.

He walked a mile to Pudding Lane,
    An old commercial street,
To the humble and long-held domain
    Of the printer Thomas Fleet.

By then a half-moon lit the night,
    No sound of horse and cart,
And Tatterjack kept out of sight
    Until he knew by heart

Each window on the second floor
    And which one marked his prey.
He started for the print-shop door . . .
    Then almost ran away.

The Faerie Queen had made him swear;
    He knew she'd not forgive
If he shirked his only purpose there
    And let the lady live.

Resolved, he spidered up the wall,
    A climber of such skill
It took him but a breath to crawl
    To Goody Goose's sill.

The goodwife lay inside, abed,
    And many were her years;
A foulness 'twas to strike her dead,
    And muffle screams from ears,

For even in her sleep she sang
    The rhymes that children love;
They brought to Tatterjack a pang,
    His mother's face above:

*Hush-a-bye, baby, on the tree top,*
    *When the wind blows the cradle will rock;*
*When the bough breaks the cradle will fall,*
    *Down will come baby, cradle, and all.*

Although to do so he was loath,
    And caused his heart to race,
He pressed a pillow's straw and cloth
    To Mother Goose's face.

Now that the deed was done he fled,
    A phantom in the night,
And as the crooning crone was dead,
    He hoped as well his plight.

Inside his pocket was a ball,
    An orb of crystal glass,
So he the Faerie Queen might call
    And tell what came to pass.

He glimpsed her face, her garnet crown:
    "Your task is incomplete,
For Fleet has set the verses down
    Upon a printed sheet."

He wished to rage, yet stayed his voice;
    No anger would she brook.
He saw no other earthly choice
    But burn Fleet's evil book.

Come day, the corpse was carted off.
    A fever then was rife;
What started as a simple cough
    Could end a person's life.

Old Mother Goose was laid to rest,
    A headstone for her grave,
And Tatterjack, he thought it best
    To wait it out, the knave.

A week he lingered. Then he struck.
    "Sir, should your shop require
A printer's devil, you're in luck,"
    Fibbed Tatterjack, the liar.

Against his better judgment, Fleet
    Did hire that crooked man:
"You look a vagrant off the street;
    I'll take though what I can."

With chills his servant boy was sick,
    His family deep in grief,
And so he, blinded to the trick,
    Fell victim to the thief.

Then day by day did Tatterjack
    Set letters by the score;
A printer's devil, stained in black,
    He relished well his chore.

His element he'd found at last,
    An eel beneath the sea.
None inked the letters half so fast;
    Content for once was he.

And once his master's trust was earned,
    He made a bold request,
Though with a laugh his plea was spurned,
    For Fleet thought it a jest:

That he forgo the book of verse,
    His dam-in-law's writ down,
For printing it would bring a curse
    And lose Queen Mab her crown.

Though Tatterjack cajoled and knelt,
    His master's heart was hard;
A devil's bargain he was dealt,
    A hand without a card.

The books, once leather-bound and sewn,
    Were sorted stack by stack.
"Sell twenty volumes on your own,"
    Said Fleet to Tatterjack,

Who stuffed a satchel with the lot
    And trod to Merchants Hall,
But wouldn't let one book be bought,
    Absconded with them all.

He thought to burn them up in fire,
    Yet reasoned that the sea
Might satisfy the Queen's desire
    And even set him free.

The docks again, all gulls and rats,
    With not a merry soul,
Were perfect for the alley cats
    That trailed our Old King Cole.

Those cats became a mob of brats
    In homespun dark with fleas.
To Tatterjack they doffed their hats,
    As polished as you please.

Although the man was twice as large,
    A boy removed his pack;
Another made a sudden charge
    And toppled Tatterjack.

The urchins, quick as fiddles, left
    Him flopping like a fish,
Too weak to chase them, too bereft,
    As the spoon pursued the dish.

He knew he was defeated now,
    By children and by fate;
No way was left to keep his vow;
    He felt his failure's weight.

Like dandelion seeds would spread
    The rhymes across new lands,
Although he'd killed their bringer dead
    With pale and clammy hands.

Though once a man was Tatterjack,
    To Faerie had he strayed;
For him there was no turning back;
    The Queen would not be swayed.

He took revenge before he fled,
    To vaunt his great disdain,
And stole the stone that marked the head
    Of her whom he had slain.

# Gaia's Prophecy

*John Shirley*

The human crowd is chattering
Unhearing men trade flattering;
Those ever speaking cannot hear
The voice of the Unseen One near

But quiet ones hear the unheard
Echolocation bears their words:
Spirits of trees, the spirits of mammals;
*Animae Mundi* of all animals

Spirits of caverns, spirits of sea:
Their moaning cries echo to me—
They mourn the loss of mermaid daughters;
Of fish and whales, dolphins and otters

In forest is heard the lamentation
For creatures lost in mass extinction;
And birds are dying as insects vanish,
Seeds are gone or cease to nourish

All things reduced to digital dots
In mankind's snare are biomes caught;
I hear dryads wail to the High:
Asking why and why—and why

At last is come sweet Gaia's answer
She flicks a finger at the cancer:
"The humans corrupt with greed and hurry
Have turned the seas to plastic slurry

"They choke Poseidon, and elementals,
Burn up nature's fundamentals;
More than locusts, more than mold
They gulp and blight all they behold

"But harken to this prophesy:
Their works will fall to entropy;
When all is guzzled by their greed
On each other they will feed

"Humanity will consume itself:
A new extinction on the shelf;
In five hundred turns 'round the sun,
All men and women will be gone

"Then shall the world regenerate:
Rise to invest the insensate;
Forests once more will effloresce
Fireflies will incandesce

"Snakes will glitter, penguins flash
Spouting whales through waves crash;
Unknown species will emerge
In time to struggle and diverge

"My kaleidoscope will whirl in glory
And up will rise a newborn story:
Nature returns to sanity—
And I won't bring back humanity."

# Echoing Dylan Thomas; or, A Cri de Cœur from Reader to Writer

*Carl E. Reed*

My favorite writers keep dying—goddamn!
Punch to the gut, gasp of the heart.
How dare they slip from life to death?
Immortal! Immortal! cried their art.

True, legions of writers were dead when I burst
red-faced from the womb, writhing in fear;
the solace I took for having been born:
great books that I read fell year-upon-year.

Yet writers entombed in green-grassed graves
or whited sepulchers that shine o'er bright
in the eros-glare of the nurturing sun
struck me as fair; struck me as right.

But living writers? Who jape, love & laugh
weep & console, thunder & rage—
protean spirits of wondrous writ words
e'en such as these—The Greats of the page

surrender—at end—to devouring void.
Do not go gentle into that good night!

grief-stricken poet Dylan Thomas cried:
Rage, rage 'gainst the dying . . . light!

*Postscript:*
Shadows elongate; flesh shuddereth.
Anon. Alas!
Anon.

# That Was Epic

*Maxwell I. Gold*

Forged in awful plastic cities, remnant pieces of something that once was flesh decayed in rust and ruined philosophies, displaced across some random-access memory points. These placated realities, the broken choices and discarded bodies were the awful remembrances of a society huddled in the shadow of monstrous greed; engorged by the light of progress, too late until the dirges rang o'er the muddied streets under limp metal towers when the skies let loose an awesome and terrible wrath.

Felled by some unreasonable doom, metallic limbs, fiery eyes, and blackened, twisted iron branches slammed into the earth. Bits and brain-like matter grayed in the clouds of yesterday covered the ashy surface of the world. And too late, were the naïve insects who crawled along the thin nimble crust of the world; captivated by the falling stars that wrapped everything in dancing ribbons of heat and a sour, tangerine, aurorean splendor.

Piles of sand turned to glass, and oceans of gold and salt constituted a new, almost alien terrain where the columns of plastic and steel were vaporized in the final moments as the old, yellow star bellowed one last time . . . *That was epic.*

# Reading by Ghost Light

### Dmitri Akers

Lunacy grew with the spread of fair *Selene*: aglow on a pale page,
Elder things stirred from the words of a dead Poet, children of night-
    time,
*Nyx* was there, dancing to Hadean hymns, under spectrums of ghost
    light,
Horrors there hovered and circled 'round, o'er dusty leaves of some
    black books.
Gates to *Elysium* oped with Tartarean stench of long dead gods,
Billowing out, dreads on wings tittered and screeched as they flew high,
Spiralling upwards, a phantasmic fountain of deadened and lost souls,
Glyphs of some language infernal had seared maledictions on blank
    white.

# How Love Fled

### *Simon MacCulloch*

> "I think it proves very definitely that Madame Delambre was quite insane."—George Langelaan, "The Fly"

I'm hunting a fly with the head of a man.
I'm hunting a fly with the head of my husband.
My kitchen's a butcher shop, bloody red meat.
It ought to attract him. He doesn't come home.
The others come, hungry. Their heads are all black.
I crush all their maggots before they can sprout.
I coax in the spiders, patrol all the webs.
The spiders grow fat on the black-headed swarm.
I know that he's hiding himself in the crowd.
He thinks when I catch him I'll pull off his wings.
I listen for words in the scissoring buzz.
We love you, we love you, they're trying to say.
I sleep smeared with honey, they crawl on my dreams.
A golden-sweet woman. They suckle my skin.
We love you, they say with their glittering eyes,
We love you, we love you, our queen of the flies.

# Moonfog

*Wade German*

Slowly, the dreams of dusk are drawn
    Within the nebulous black field
        That seethes above with spectral stars,
        Which part like floating nenuphars
As crawling out its crypt to dawn
    The corpse-green moon becomes revealed:

Risen, it lurks through lakes of cloud;
    Its wake is trailing veils of mist
        Which drift like ghosts, descending on
        The valley, forest, hill and lawn
To weave the village in a shroud,
    The graveyard bound within its midst:

Where gelid, green-lit glowing fog
    By curling plume and tendril creeps:
        Invading tombs through cracks and seams,
        Inducing every corpse to dream,
Anointed thus with hypnagogue . . .
    And dead things walk from dreamless sleep.

# Anathema

*Lori R. Lopez*

Born on the coldest night in a hundred years,
straight from the womb into a frigid embrace,
the first puff of air contracted chills and frost
to dangle frozen. The baby laughed at her
magical gust. But a midwife abandoned both
corpse and child to feed the Grimmerwolves—
instead, pounced upon by a bristling pack!

The babe cooed and gurgled with delight.

Anathema was she named by foulest wind,
and the curse that lingered on a mother's lips.
Her savage spirit would in runes be cast—
while tips of quills spelled out in scratches
of strange ungodly ruminations and cravings;
from madness and ruthless crawlings of flesh,
that all detest a Were-Lass raised by beasts.

Merrily pranced she, a sylvan sprite.

Pagan blood, with neither claim nor blame
to being a Bête Noire. Bound in her eldritch
sanctum of unlight, the chasmic bosom of
Nocturne. Within her fortress abyss in deepest
dark, a sheltered cave surrounded by serene

shy forest of ancient growths, eldest timbers
impervious to blade—a secret enclave.

There played she, the picture of sweet.

For Malice and Woe—preternatural
elements of Ill Fortune—could not be
inherited; they must be earned, desired,
accumulated over decades of communion
with the prime-evilest occult gatherings.
Such could not be gained a single night . . .
despite the shape or disposition of a moon.

Yet Ana romped with wildest abandon!

Half-untamed, half-childish she cavorted.
Sporting and frolicking; learning, coveting
Wolven Ways; taught the lessons of Weald
and Bush, the laws of Nature and Alpha.
Though she was soft and dainty as petals,
Anathema would rule with claw and tooth.
Until a dire reputation preceded footsteps.

An abundance of gleeful rampages!

Six daring youths set out to capture just
a glimpse, then ran to share a taller tale:
how Ana with her snarling Hell-Brutes
tried to slash and devour the boys alive!
Truthful or not; a Hunting Party formed,
embarking on raging steeds, charging
toward the pitchblack woodland heart.

Anathema heard a thunderous pulse . . .

Semi-hypnotic, half-animated, hollow.
There seemed no place to go but delve
the glummest insidious-most reaches . . .
treading lines between morbidly cracked
and potently bittersweet, twisted or gifted
by magnificent senses . . . crossed over by
the aptest, keenest, quickest of instincts.

Darting on wolf toes as the crows did fly.

Loathed and roundaboutly dreaded, she!
Villainesse, Grimmerwolf Queen, Witch
of Briar and Bramble Patches, howling
and prowling her domain, Ana did not

retreat in fear. She sought no battle,
deserved neither punishment nor reward,
only that an uneasy truce remain . . .

All joy forever lost, her Pack defended.

A single man limped home in warning:
*Do not go near this woman's world.*

# The Gorgon Queen

*Ron L. Johnson II*

Your serpentine glance
Freezes my breath,
Which rapidly fogs,
And then freezes
Like a lance.

Through me
Your gaze goes
through me.

You are the Gorgon
That stoned my heart
With a glance.

# The Savage Fantasies of Mr. Arbuthnot

*Manuel Pérez-Campos*

With exhausting minuteness I-95 reminisces
in silence along with him in the nycthemeral
frame of his van's rear view mirror the last
words of underpass hitchhikers who have
undergone live burial in deep wood as he sought
from them in vain the magic word that would
make him stop, just as he was once unable
to find it when his father, that lout of a much
admired churchman, cancelled an ambition
to remain unnoticed by would-be tormentors
by shutting him two years in a shed: mightier
than Morpheus is his brother, and like
that brother no one likes to think about
is he, despite a crewcut silver-flamed: he
relishes entering their hearts like a shadow
that will never leave as he toys with their bribed
imaginations, to let them think they will escape.

# After Heathcliff Digs Up Cathy

*Michael Potts*

He takes Cathy's body in his arms,
pulling her close, but no warmth
no gentle thump of her heart greets—
only stillness and a hint of rot.

Heathcliff ponders his life, dead
like Cathy's corpse, and he pictures
her alone, seeking the man she loved,
who failed to see, jealousy leading
him to evil, searing Cathy's heart.

In madness he hopes she revives, offers
him lips to kiss, a voice to sweeten
his dreams, but all he sees is the shape
of a dead face, its mouth held fast
by a handkerchief tied to her head,
as if stopping an eternal scream.

# The Doom

*Geoffrey Reiter*

To know the crest could crush you, for the ocean
In currents, serpentine, and rushing waves,
Bodes broken bones and broken souls, the motion
Transforming raging riptides into graves;
To see the dragon-guarded summit rise
Through glowering lightning-threaded thundercloud
Sublime in high morose ascent to skies
And echoes of their roars resound aloud;
To learn the burning bleak black blank of space
Its empty desolation and its dearth,
The dwindling spinning specks of special space
Each whirling world a microscopic earth;
To know, to see, to learn this truth is doom
If all the cosmos fall within this gloom.

# The Monsters of the Moor

(An Old Scotsman's Tale, Related in a Pub in Edinburgh on the Eve of the Great War, Winter 1914)

## Frank Coffman

*An awful beast roamed o'er the moor, a horror to behold,*
*For what, but one short hour before, had been a man was man no more,*
*Leaving a trail of blood and gore—or so the story's told.*

"Come ye brave laddies. Gather 'round. A grim tale I will tell.
More frightful a story canna be found. A Thing of Evil loose, unbound
Stalked our moorlands and forest ground. A Creature set free from Hell.

"'Twas in the year of '52," the frail, pale gaffer said.
"I swear to you my tale is true. Its trail was terrible to view,
 For, come the morning, a blood-red dew circled the gruesome dead!

"The Beast would prowl when the moon was round, and, come the
    morrow morn,
Many a grisly corpse was found, in forest deep or heathered ground,
With mangled limbs, deep, ghastly wounds, the bodies ripped and torn.

"At first, most said, 'A madman's spree! And we must find him fast!
Of this lunatic's scourge we must be free!' But it was proof to some—*and me*—
And, very soon, most did agree—before three months had passed.

"The timing, the horrid deaths made clear—a *Werewolf* walked the moor!
And each full moon was time for fear. On the night wind wild howls
    we'd hear.

In heather, in wood, by deep, dark mere, the lands were soaked with
    gore!

"I was only a lad of eighteen when I gladly joined the quest
  To hunt the beast 'cross moor and fen, track it over hill and glen,
  Find it and somehow kill it then. Just how no one had guessed.

"When next was full the Old Man's Face, we gathered in the town,
  We spread out from that meeting place, quite sure that we would find its
    trace,
  Give out the signal and give chase and hunt that Terror down.

"Old Angus, Ewan, Tom, and I, set out toward the East.
  Its howl we heard, and, by and by, its strange, clawed footprints we did
    spy.
  Four of us followed, but three would die! victims of the Beast.

"Lads, I've seen many a bloody sight. In The Crimea that next year
  We Black Watch fought in many a fight, and I claim to be brave by right,
  But the carnage I saw on that dread night! . . . Any man would quake
    with fear.

"I did *more than my share* of bloody deeds, those years I spent at war.
  And a man will do what the moment needs, wherever the trail of survival
    leads,
  And the consequences he no longer heeds, as he was wont before.

"Well, we found the trail of that Man-Wolf fell. Tom fired a signal shot.
 But that wasted round was Tom's death knell. And Angus and then
    Ewan fell.
That creature, truly the Spawn of Hell, had tracked *us* to the spot.

"My only weapon—me dad's old cane, with a silver knob at its head,
 It turned to me, and full amain, it charged! I struck it again and again,
'Til it screamed out with a howl of pain—then fell at my feet, stone dead!

"Then I watched in horror as its form did change, from a wolf back to a
    man!
A transformation, indeed, most strange. I watched its features rearrange,
The body of wolf and man exchange! Imagine, if you can!

"By the time the others reached the place, a dead man there did lie,
 With bludgeon wounds on his head and face. And of a wolf, there was
    no trace.
'Twas a curséd human, fallen from Grace. But a man like you or I.

"Well that's my tale, and I swear it's truth. I care not if you believe.
 I was but eighteen but I say, in sooth, that was the last night of my youth.
 My heart's been laden with heavy ruth. For *humankind* I grieve.

"*That night* and the following years of war, have left me with scant hope.
 Nothing is now as it was before. Peace is a thing I knew of yore.

And now I'm nearing the Last Great Door. For the Light, I've ceased to grope.

"And now a greater war I fear, is soon to touch us all.
I'm eighty; I won't live out the year. But you, my lads, drink up your beer.
War's thunder I hear in my memory's ear. And some of you shall fall."

But part of his tale was left untold on that dark, disquieting night.
The gravest detail did he withhold—that on that night, as the full moon rolled,
That he, as a youth full brave and bold, *had suffered the creature's bite!*

The gaffer turned, and he left the place, leaving the lads in awe.
There wasn't a smile on any face. His warning words they couldn't erase.
Two followed, but they could find no trace! 'Twas the last of him they saw.

That summer brought the guns of war, the wide world's Greatest Fight.
Nothing would be as it was before. Bombs from the sky and the cannon's roar.
But still could be heard howls on the moor—a werewolf stalked by night.

*An awful beast roams o'er the moor, a horror to behold,*
*For what, but one short hour before, was just a man is man no more,*
*Leaving a trail of blood and gore—and stories will be told.*

# In Lakewood Cemetery

*Tylor James*

In Lakewood Cemetery
Some have spoke an eerie sight;
That of creature or fairy—
They roost in the trees at night.

They roost in the trees at night;
Shadow-blotches on the moon.
They bend the branches in flight;
Gliding over path and tomb.

Some say they are vultures
Some suggest they are owls
Others claim they are sculptures—
Resurrected gargoyles!

Ever since a young child,
I have desired to know
The truth; be it strange or mild—
What flies beneath the moonglow?

What flies beneath the moonglow;
Pale as the surrounding tombs?
What makes the dark shadows grow
O'er those crypts and vaults of gloom?

\*

Many a day I have strolled through
The endless graves and mausoleums,
Till in my heart a melancholy grew
And I fell in love with Death's Museum,

Whose artifacts are eternal;
Names and dates carved in marble stone;
And the wind that blows is charnel;
whispers of worm and wind and bone!

Whispers of worm and wind and bone;
For these are the Voices of the Dead
That stir one's soul when one's alone;
Attuned to that music borne of dread.

I hunkered down in shadowed groves of dusk,
Until the rusty iron gates clanged shut.
When the moon raised high its white crescent tusk,
I heard something *crack!*–like twig or chestnut.

Like twig or chestnut—I heard something *crack!*
I peered above the gravestones at the sight
Of snarling demons garbed in hooded black—
Beware, beware! Those who roost in the trees at night!

Their vermillion eyes glow with angry fire;
O, how I gazed in awe at their horrid height!
For they grinned wide with teeth like razor wire;
Those *fiends!* Those *fiends* that roost in the trees at night!
Linger not, I pray, in midnight's pale-frozen day;
For it is better to be smart, wise, and wary.
For now, alas, I have but one last thing to say:
One must tread softly in Lakewood Cemetery.

# Sacred

*Lee Clark Zumpe*

I uttered the words—
hesitantly—
as my trembling finger
traced sacred esoteric teachings
across yellowed, cracked parchment.

I articulated the invocation—
Passionately—
pronouncing blasphemies
with a degree of intimacy
reserved for the names of secret lovers.

I shuddered with satisfaction—
Triumphantly—
as their voices multiplied,
engulfing my meager chant
with howls of the damned.

# vampire dragon: a haiku

*Kendall Evans*

the sleeping dragon
        sucks sustenance
                from a dying virgin's
nightmarish dreams

# The Great and Final Feast

*Jay Sturner*

Eyes blur open to crepuscular gray. Air hot, humid, pungent with unfamiliar rot. Lanky, bat-winged forms soar high overhead. Lying on my back, I try to get up, am held static by an unyielding suction of damp earth. Fleshy lumps lean and hiss from every angle. What is this place? If a dream it is all too real, and far beyond my imaginative capabilities. No time to wonder: a glittering wall of crimson rock, rising into tumorous gray clouds, groans and cracks ominously in the distance. I twist, turn, grunt in protest. At length I unlatch myself from the ground, leap to my feet. The flying things swoop low, circle about, their many-horned heads beaming green, torch-like eyes—a dozen tiny spotlights racing across my body.

    The distant, monolithic wall splits apart horizontally in zigzag aspect—the lower half remaining terrestrial while the other lifts into the sky, raining red. I think of monstrous stalagmites and stalactites. I think of teeth. And now a bright field of stars streams in through the yawning crack. I step forward, wavering atop a layer of slime. I think of mucous on an immense tongue. One by one, unfamiliar forms sail and tumble into the great maw, some vocal, others seemingly unconscious. Moments later I'm airborne—inhaled backwards, violently, into a distant cavern.

*

Sunless blue sky. Golden sand stretching off to fleshy, veined horizons. All I can think is, *I've been swallowed.* I peer down. Random portions of my body seem . . . void of existence. Flesh droops like wet tissue paper where bones no longer exist. Attempting to shut my eyes, I realize I've no lids. Like a wounded beast I curl upon the sand, pray my soul will jettison from this dissolving body and find its way to God. In that same moment a wordless, primeval voice sears my intellect and rouses a terrible truth: That my soul will *never* escape this place, that it too will dissolve.

With biologically incomplete tongue I make yet another attempt to reach God. In response that same voice informs me that yes, my prayer *has* been answered, I *am* with God—but only because . . . *He too is here.* And worse, no longer His true self but merely a wandering thought—a series of synapses really—within the omnipresent mind of this entity. Lured, swallowed, *digested*. Along with trillions of other minds both human and otherwise.

How did this happen? What dark channel did I follow in life, what dark portal enter, to be caught like a fish unawares on some cosmic hook? Last I remember I'd been asleep in my apartment. But such questions will not be answered, for they have been made to no longer matter. Devoid of emotion, nearly unconscious, and physically unable to resist anyway, I submit to my fate.

And now I—as a disembodied, pocked head dissolving upon the golden sand—am made privy to the final, beautiful truth as it capsizes my logic and syncs with my waning awareness: That like a cannibalistic Eden feasting upon its own brilliant blooms, the Universe, in the form of this gargantuan, impossible eater, is taking itself back, unchallenged—one doomed consciousness at a time.

# Lunar Mission

### *Katherine Kerestman*

Hand-in-hand round golden rings, maidens skip,
Pink lunar dust wafts up while they keep time.
With hands-across and half-poussette they clip;
And boldly troubadours romances rhyme
With woodwind airs and thrums of lyre strings,
While swains slay dragons in the starry sky,
Embarked on quests to fetch down Saturn's rings.
Pusses-in-Boots and Ulthar cats leap nigh
To Venus, Jupiter, and warlike Mars,
Where sightless mole-men tunnel catacombs—
Spyholes—so bright blue whales may see the stars—
And Mother Goose has tea with Sherlock Holmes.
Whene'er I visit the back side of the moon,
I planet-hop, fly in my mind's balloon;
And yet (declare dull mortals made of clay)
The dark side of the moon is cold and gray.

# Beneath the Mirror Moon

*Ngo Binh Anh Khoa*

Cloaked in the silence of the chilling night
And cobwebbed by the blackened moon's pale gleam,
The mist-enshrouded wood seems like a dream
That shifts beneath the shredded threads of light.
The echo of a lost soul's footfalls rings,
Each step a heavy, agonizing sound
Within this shadowed realm where beasts abound,
And where the dark beyond the darkness sings.
Clouds part. The mirror moon—untarnished—glows,
And primal growls prowl through the quietude
From out the lengthening maw whose fangs exude
The foetid stench of death that stronger grows.
The wanderer's human guise is shed, and there,
The Werewolf howls, with hunger in its glare.

# The Torment of Flame

*Deborah L. Davitt*

My gaze is fire—
a sprawl of sparks and embers
fly out of my eyes
deadly as Medusa's glare,
my form wreathed by ashes, char:

my chains glow white-hot
against my leaden skin;
my flaming essence
seethes, searching for its release,
which the gods will never grant.

I don't know for which
    sin I've been so imprisoned,
for which misstep I
    was turned to molten shame—
    I long for liquid pity.

A single tear might
    douse this, my conflagration.
and set my soul free
    to dance upon the wind:
    Release me, mortal, I pray.

# Love Came upon a Darkling Night

*William Clunie*

I cannot stand in fearful condemnation
of much malignèd death when even now
my truest love is dead. It began
with rubbings taken from those ancient stones,
mementos of both life and loss, some dull,
some dire: the Surrey twins, eight years of age
who fell into a well (they did everything
together) and the mother who outlived
them by but three more months—the rubbings
of the angels that adorned their stones
hang now upon my chamber wall.

Perhaps that's why she came to me, poor wretch,
a lunar month in time since erst I visited
those stones, the first of daily sojourns as
I sat amongst the dead and mused upon
the short lives of those tragic twins, the mother
soon to follow, wondering how she died,
a suicide? a broken heart? Ultimately
I hung the rubbings of those cherubs
in my solitary chamber, a remembrance
on my wall of the shortness of their lives,
a memento mori of my own. Upon a time.

\* \* \*

I fell into a fitful sleep, only to
awaken to a presence at my side,
frail, pale alabaster shine of skin scant
inches from my hand. Fear and fascination
drew me close, and then away, until at last
a few brief syllables I dared to say:
"*Who are you?*" Her words came slow from milk-blue
lips, unaccustomed as they were
to speaking in the world of mortal things:
"I am the mother of those little ones
you visit in the cold hard ground," she said,
"and I am here to thank you for your deeds."

Her gratitude came quick and needful
as her bony hand reached out to me;
in my half-awakened state my reasoned self
made explanation—*this is but a dream!*—
as allowed me to partake of flesh
that seemed both hot and frozen as this
errant long-dead succubus found comfort
for a night in living arms. After eldritch
satisfaction gained I wiped away
the tears that stood on sharp gaunt cheeks,
my beating heart full aching though I felt

no corresponding tremor in her own
thin breast. "Do you sorrow that you came
to me?" She grew colder as the words wisped
out like frozen breath: *"I sorrow that I leave."*
I held her closer, chilled by flesh that had
briefly been most hot; I let her speak,
let the words release before she would be gone:
*"The things I miss:* my sweet girls' arms
around me, the pleasure of a man beside me"
(at this she clutched me tighter till I felt
a tremor seemingly more fear than lust)
"the smaller things," she carried on,
"how it would be to wash my hair again!"
At this she laughed and slow began to fade
inside my arms, her gaze no longer held
on mine but locked on those impressions,
simple and angelic, tacked upon my wall.
*"Good-bye,"* she husked, and desiccated flesh
turned to dust inside my bed.

Would that I could pass along that Charlotte,
for 'twas her name, chiseled on her headstone,
came to me night after night for years
and years, until I died a peaceful
ancient in my time and lie beside her

even still, but 'twould be a lie: Never
did I see her further. Long years have passed
but still I sit beside her grave, the mother
and her babes, remembering the glowing eyes
that looked into my own, the lover
that did come and go, that ruined me
for others, for nothing sweeter is there
than to find one's love in one's own time,
and nothing sadder is there than to lose
true love and live a life forever yet alone.

# Hic Aqua Est

*Joshua Gage*

Nobody knows the stars that haunt me.
Nobody understands my heart
is an unmapped sailor navigating the constellations
towards certain shipwreck. Nobody hears
the seductions of the waves. But I do,
I do. Now I lay me down
to sleep to escape the world. I will sink
into the quiet shadows of isolation.
I will dream until my body becomes
the water, the very ocean itself.
Sailor, prepare to drown.

# Malvolio's Revenge

### *Kyla Lee Ward*

"For Andrew, if he were opened, and you find so much blood in his liver as will clog the foot of a flea, I'll eat the rest of the anatomy."
—Sir Toby Belch, *Twelfth Night*

All appetite is sin: I see my foes
now choke upon the fruit they plucked in haste.
My mistress, who a handsome stranger chose
but knows a crop-haired woman to her taste!
Sir Toby's cakes and ale are only fit
To fat him and his slattern for the grave.
And Aguecheek, who blames his lack of wit
Upon a love of beef. And still they crave
What damns them. There's an oath the Belcher made
to eat a coward's flesh. To help him keep
his word were Christian. So, in ambuscade,
you'll mark the meat comes fresh and very cheap.
They called me mad. Now those who eat will see
And reach, perhaps, their own epiphany.

# By Creator Forsaken

*Scott J. Couturier*

Patchwork man of off-cast parts—
Sewn with stitches, made to look
Like a living thing—
Lightning lends you animacy,
Calls a soul into being,
Mismatched eyes opening as
Your mouth cries wordless,
Though you have a dead
Man's tongue & brain.
By my arcane science you see:
By my will you move, think, & breathe.
I am your inventor, your Creator,
Demiurge of your fleshly reality.
By my will alone you stir:
In fear you stare at me, fear
Or fury, an uncomprehending
Gaze that sets me trembling,
Terrified of my works in turn.

With a stagger I fall back,
Moan & flee your chamber,
Where you glare from your
Ebony slab, glare & mouth dumbly,
Of your restraints not yet aware.
Soon to struggle, as every creature must—

You shall free yourself at last
& leave this castle, leave me
Who made you, stitched you
Together tenderly in those long,
Dreadful watches of night!
Yet I feel sick fear at sight of you:
Feel the blasphemy of my ambitions.
Thus I must forsake you, Creation,
To a world obscene,
Your maker absent even as God is
From His patchwork children of stolen
Heart & bone, soul & dream.

# Grave-Robbing 2.0: Intermediate

*Darrell Schweitzer*

So why are we digging *him* up,
after it took so long to get him into the ground?
We thought he'd live forever,
infinitely powerful, evil, wise, learned,
always onto our conniving schemes,
who only let us go on living
out of some incomprehensible whim,
like a cat toying with wounded mice.
No, I won't shut up. Over the wall we go,
across the lawn in the moonlight, shovels rattling.
The last thing I'm worried about is the police.
Jail, an asylum, would seem like paradise.
Tell me again why we are doing this.
For ghoulish baubles? A talisman?
An intriguing ring with a finger still in it?
If he was buried with a book, it must be
a sodden mass by now.
If you're planning some kind of rite,
it may not be such a good idea.
Please reconsider.
The coffin lid splintered with surprising ease.
Now you've done it!
That shriveled, grinning face!

You snatch the coins off his eyes.
They're open!
Now you're consumed in raging flame,
without even time to scream,
while I go quietly mad.

Master, I serve you always, with love and loyalty,
though I admit I am very much afraid.

# A Vision of Carcosa

## David C. Kopaska-Merkel

We are practicing the invocation. By tomorrow evening we must be perfect. A damp rag wipes the belly clean. The aromatic smoke lazily coiling from the brazier makes me cough.

"Again!"

Bold strokes; I drag the lump of coal left to right, curve the terminus just so. Symbols, left pelvis, navel, and rib cage edge. It's done! A greater darkness billows from the ceiling. Lightning strikes the sacrifice; he screams. A projection of the cloud caresses his face.

"The wards," I shout, but Roger's face shows that he forgot.

the lake
a suckered tentacle
curls around my calf

# The Night of Mirth and Magic

*Andrew White*

Deep within the dead of night,
When mad witches take their flight,
Shadows come to life and bite—
Samhain is upon us!

Dance the skeleton dance,
Join the gypsy in her trance,
Watch the restless spirits prance—
The Hallowed Eve has come!

A day of treat, a night of tricks,
Candles burn down to their wicks,
Monsters beings get their kicks—
Celebrate but be on guard!

Come, my friends, and join the fray,
Today is not just any day,
A time for ghouls and ghosts to play—
The night of mirth and magic!

# There upon the Threshold

*Carl E. Reed*

Pitiless life grinds pain-wracked flesh to grit
    pitted, scarred & loose the weathered husk
of desiccated puppet: brittle boned
    collapse-clatter-rattle-gasp in dark'ning dusk.

Gentling death advances with a sigh
    & rustle of silken robes—offers hand
white as maggots bursting from the rot
    frothed from lips frost-blued in Netherland.

I reach up—fevered, thirsting, limbs a-tremble
    to grasp proffered kindly, killing claw—
sibilant hiss of nihilist cold abyss
    annihilating dread. Ah! Greater awe!

# Telos Falling

*Maxwell I. Gold*

Past the worst impossibilities were the indescribable choices that lay waiting at the bottom of tomorrow. The corpse that was Hope twitched and sighed in the voided dark of my bruised and bloodied brain—drained of matter or truth like the empty streets of that ancient city that once towered over everything including my own bleak perceptions. Great structures hewn from plastic and neuron-limbs climbed and reached toward the most infinite, scar-tissue ceiling where I swore the stars begged me to jump, to fall into the lumpy graveyard where Hope waited.

I'd knew I'd been here before, consumed with the anxiety of choice, a familiar and depressing compunction that filled my thoughts like viridescent noxious clouds. Soon everything was forfeit, my choice and my body, collapsed onto itself as if the city suffered its doom by the awful rust from crooked teeth.

Gnawing at the foundations of Everything, I was smashed and swallowed into the pits below where no possibilities existed only the swirling, black mass of ambivalence which throbbed beneath a milky, brain-fogged spectral radiance—my corpse at the bottom of tomorrow buried with Hope.

# Daughters of Phorcys

*Wade German*

### I. THE GREY ONES

The three sisters sat at the mouth of their cave, passing their one eye between them. Enyo had been gazing with the eye longer than usual, so her siblings asked what she could see.

"Civilization come all at once to a standstill, as if hearkening to whispered doctrines of destruction." She then handed the eye to Pemphredo, who in her turn, also gazed with the eye a little longer than usual. So her siblings asked her what she could see.

"People, entire populaces, as if maddened by the perpetual pipes of Pan, each infected by a fungal growth of ever-spreading panic and fear." She then passed the eye into the hand of Deino. She, too, gazed with it longer than usual. So her siblings asked what she could see.

"The decayed sun, guttering until it glows no more. Like a dead lamp, it swings in the winds of the void, shedding only an ensorcelled darkness on worlds that weep, each alone in the cosmic cold, and they whimper without hope of succour."

For a long time, they gurgled together in mirth. Then they began passing their one tooth between them, each taking turn at sucking blood from the wide-eyed waif who stood spellbound before them, and thrice-sealed the augured dooms.

## II. PEMPHREDO IN THE MARSH

Grown weary from conjuring spirits, and hungered by unwanted fasting, Pemphredo handed the eye to her sisters and made her way into the marshes.

She stalked blindly into the brackish waters until knee-deep, then stood completely still, listening intently to the harmonious *brekekekèx-koàx-koáx* of the frogs. Sensing one near, she snatched it up with the precision of a heron, and gorged upon it.

She fed like this into the crepuscular hour, when the waters began to churn. Then with a terrific splash, an enormous frog leapt before her, croaking a dismal dirge.

Pemphredo cried: "Oh, Monarch of the Marshes, I take only a few from your innumerable brood!" And in the primordial, beautifully alien syllables of the batrachians, she began to croon an ancient song of praise to the Mother of Frogs.

Seemingly appeased by this oblation, the goddess retreated lugubriously through the reeds, and sank into the waters from whence she came. With belly distended, Pemphredo found her way back to her sisters, who were busy dragging corpses out of graves.

## III. ENYO

On clear evenings when the moon had refused all visitation to the heavens, and when her sisters were asleep, it was Enyo's custom to take up the eye and set forth on a solitary ramble through the hills.

From a dark prominence, she could see the white shapes of the buildings in the city below, which was surrounded by a nighted sea. Then she would hail and invoke the names of certain spheres that hold certain influences over the minds of men.

When her invocations were over, and she could perceive the floating layer of dreams that spread like a blanket over the sleeping city, she would crouch like a spider and begin weaving spells into the metaphysic fabric of those dreams.

And all who slept in the city dreamt things which disturbed them, whether they would remember them or not; but those who remembered were forever gripped by the talons of black chimeras, and inevitably dissolved into madness and death.

## IV. DEINO

Of the three sisters it was Deino who was most proficient in the art of herbal lore, and in the course of practicing that occupation she had become addicted to certain drugs.

Her lips were always laced with a tincture of oleander, and her breath was the odour of belladonna. By moonlight, her eyes glowed with the greenish-yellow tint of wormwood. Her fingertips were permanently stained by the purple blood of aconite.

She would spend countless hours in the back of her cavern preparing rare herbs, extracting oils and essences, and adjusting the potencies of elixirs, poisonous concoctions, and the hallucinogenic potions that were so essential to her sisterhood of sorcery.

But it was only she that used the dust of an exotic compound that she crushed especially from night-blooming flowers and the organs of certain nocturnal creatures. Even when eyeless, it enabled her to see beyond the night sky and into unknown worlds, which for a while, were hers alone for the knowing.

## V. THREE HAGS UNDER THE HORNS OF HECATE

The three sisters sat at the mouth of their cave as the moon, enormously gravid and blood red, rose on the horizon.

The three took turns ladling mouthfuls of a thick green substance from a small cauldron set before them. As they slurped at the soup—a mélange of dreams and nightmares, herbal narcotics and hallucinatory spices, and some gobbets of frog meat—there was a palpable sense of anticipation amongst them.

Then a crescent-shaped shadow began to creep across the face of the moon, slowly shading it an even more sombre shade of red; and by incremental adumbration, the aspect of the lunar surface became that of a horned giant's skull: severed and bloody, a vast and floating phantasm in space.

"It has begun! It has begun!" the three screeched hideously in ecstatic unison. And they continued to screech: at first in awful elation, but then with a stranger, ancient voice of evil adulation; and the night winds carried their shrieks around the surrounding hills and into the sable sky.

Then there was a sheen in the welkin, like that of a spiderweb seen by a cryptic glimmer of starlight: a thin tissue of some metaphysic fabric, and it spread across the entire firmament.

And something moved behind it.

It was in this manner that after countless eons, the three sisters called forth something horrible; a thing that had been unable to resolve itself into reality on its own.

# Ravensong

*Lori R. Lopez*

Rows of umbral mourners aligned as drab adorners
Mistaken for ranks of crows . . . similar in nose
Resembling birds of a feather, angels from the nether
Boasting wings and airspeeds; diving into murky deeds
Perched like bats reversed. Dreaded as if cursed

Sinister as spies . . . clad in general Corvus guise
Huddled at a coterie; dressed for Espionagery
In shiny midnight coats with tails and inky gloats
Hunched on wires and boughs, haughtier-than-thous
Or standing in a crowd, dismal-draped and proud

Complaining voices deep; braying lost as sheep
The ravings of a clan seem absent scheme or plan
Protesting at the moon . . . demented as a loon
Their witty banter traded; a broodful mood or jaded
Mocking like a jay, yet plotting secrets to betray.

A Ravensong is heard from a complicated bird
Who croaks at dusk and dawn, an elegy to carrion
No merry airy trill from a shorter sweeter bill
With razor beak and tongue, a funeral dirge is sung
In satin suit she struts, a work of nerve and guts . . .

The diva of the choir. Black robes around a pyre
Bickering dark herds competing for last words
Listen to them "Tock!" Their voices rule the clock
How starkly ravens sing, in tune as church bells ring
The bristling morbid souls collect ungodly tolls.

# Of Shapeshifters Spawned by the Revolution

*Manuel Pérez-Campos*

When the common life is incompatible
with the balustraded gardens of Versailles
the misted bosk boles sounding the autumn-
dyed voicefulness of a converging pack run—
swiftfooted, coarse, canescent—of wolves
who are not the same sombrous people
who attended church this cloudburst-prone
blackbird-troubled morning becomes the ground
of a new reality: ours a devil's sonata
of enchanted sinew and bone intent
on the destruction of an aristocratic soul
exteriorized as a redcoated concubine
who has already lost her bonnet and whose
gamboge hair billows indecorously from
bedizened steed, as though earth in releasing her
from itself had committed an error, and on possessing
with every atom of our being the smell of her urine
coursing down the pommel as she stands awkwardly
and shrieks for aid from distant fireworks
that is not forthcoming: as though having turned
a seminal corner in a dark book while terror
makes her skin—already subpar
from overzealous lute-string corset to prevent

such as us from depriving her of her womb,
that innate magical principle with which she seeks
to complicate a dynasty—lurid
because half a ravine away from being a ghost.

# Sea Dream

## Simon MacCulloch

"The sea can bind us to her many moods."
—R. H. Barlow, "The Night Ocean"

The night is alive in the ocean
Tumultuous entropy, corpse-tossing frenzy of dreams
Turned dark as the sky when the sun has been shorn of its beams
And sunk; and the gluttonous motion
Converts us to froth on the crests of the inrushing waves
Depriving the living of life and the dying of graves
Demanding a fearful devotion.

The ocean in sunlight, still dreaming
But now of the godhood of senses exalted to blend
And bask in the glittering flood of a day without end
A nurturing universe, teeming
A womb of primeval contentment around and above
Endowing the dying with life and the living with love
Through which our fulfilment comes streaming.

So yield to the ancient persistence
Of taking and giving, of darkness and light—it's a tide
Uniting whatever's within with whatever's outside
A surge into intimate distance
Erasing the lines that we draw in the sand of our thought
The awesome event in which living and dying are caught
The ocean that dreams us: existence.

# Dark Sister

*Lee Clark Zumpe*

    Down,
through wispy raven mists
she descends, endlessly,
when the world around
is black as the pit.

Gracefully she glides
through tarns of gathering gloom
huddled solicitously close to
the heart of twilight.

Her breath is frostbitten,
her voice an arctic whisper
of intricate ice crystals
murmuring ageless secrets.

This Dark Sister
gathers her forlorn disciples:
the exiles and outcasts—
grateful for her favor—

congregate at her temple,
eager to oblige her appetite
when the sun is driven
    down.

# Infernal Nocturne

### *Ngo Binh Anh Khoa*

The midnight hour nearer comes
As silence like a cancer spreads
Across the woods in darkness drowned,
Where no sane mortal dares to tread.

And once the wan-faced moon peeks through
The parted curtains of dark clouds,
The hoots of owls and caws of crows
Then shred the quietude, maddening, loud.

The wind becomes a cackling squall
That lashes out at shivering leaves,
The autumn air grows cruelly cold,
From whose harsh grip, there's no reprieve.

And when the witching hour strikes,
The shadows cast by birds and beasts
Beneath the waxen mirror moon
Are from their borrowed forms released.

They start to writhe and shift and stand
And back to humanoid shapes return.
Their wings and claws form spindly hands
While beaks and snouts to noses turn.

Right at the center of the woods,
A fire burns, around which dance
The witches, Satan's concubines,
Who hum and hiss and chant and prance.

They speak the wicked Serpent's tongue,
They praise the legions of fell Fiends,
They curse at all Creation's gifts,
Their bare flesh bathed in pale moonbeams.

They sing and dance in circle till
The flame erupts into a tower,
From which a Goat with pitch-black fur
Appears, exuding evil power.

At once, the witches kneel and bow
Before the Beast that upright stands,
Whose lengthened shade looms far and wide,
Enveloping the quivering land.

He speaks, and they in reverence heed
Each word He pours into their ears.
Moved by their wild, insatiable lust,
Toward His embrace, they all draw near.

The sounds of flesh on flesh mix with
The screams and shrieks and grunts and groans
That make the woodland creatures flee
As they in pain and ecstasy moan.

Throughout the long and blasphemous night,
Their consummation rages on
Till each witch bears the Beast's foul seeds
And warps away at break of dawn.

Back in their quaint, idyllic towns,
They'd raise the things wrought by their tryst,
Each dreaming of the promised Throne
As Mother to the Antichrist.

# The Skeleton Dance

*Joshua Green*

I stood between two graves and looked beyond,
Into a clump of barren trees at dusk.
Two geese then moaned and warned me from the pond,
To flee the pallid thing that seeks a husk.

A scent then wended down the path, a musk
Of death so sweet it tempted and entranced.
So down I walked and lifted each tree's tusk,
Until I found the man of bones that danced.

He paid no heed to me, nor even glanced,
As my own flesh began to rip away,
To form around this thing of bones that pranced,
My skin then wrapped upon himself by day.

Now here alone I dance within the glade,
Awaiting souls to come and make a trade.

# Classic Reprints

# A Dream

## William Sharp

Last night thro' a haunted land I went,
Upon whose margins Ocean leant
    Waveless and soundless save for sighs
That with the twilight airs were blent.

And passing, hearing never stir
Of footfall, or the startled whirr
    Of birds, I said, "In this land lies
Sleep's home, the secret haunt of her."

And then I came upon a stone
Whereon these words were writ alone,
    *The soul who reads, its body dies*
Far hence that moment without moan.

And then I knew that I was dead,
And that the shadow overhead
    Was not the darkness of the skies
But that from which my soul had fled.

[From Sharp's *Romantic Ballads and Poems of Phantasy* (London: Walter Scott, 1888).]

# Fog

*Mary C. Shaw*

A spectre is the fog,
Its clammy fingers thin and gray
Strangle the golden sunny day:
It stills the young one's laughter bold,
Stiffens the marrow of the old.

Across the sea fog throws a veil,
It loves the dying sailor's wail;
For ghoul and thug it clouds the light,
Makes blacker still the darkest night.

Fog covers murder, hides the gore;
And when its evil deeds are o'er
It slinks in pallid wisps to glide
Where slimy creatures slip and slide.
Foul spectre is the fog!

[First published in *Weird Tales* 24, No. 6 (December 1934): 96.]

# Reviews

# Mythology and Cosmicism

*S. T. Joshi*

MAXWELL I GOLD. *anOther Mythology: Poems*. Houston: Interstellar Flight Press, 2023. 62 pp. $14.99 tpb.

Maxwell I. Gold is no stranger to the pages of *Spectral Realms*, as his evocative prose poems have graced its pages for some years. The main thrust of these works is a focus on the potential (and actual) dangers of our over-technologized society, as Gold puts on stage a succession of "cyber gods" who destroy our humanity and render us the helpless pawns of their cosmic degradation. The prose poems in this volume—none of which have appeared in *Spectral Realms*—have a somewhat different orientation. Here Gold has seized upon Greek mythology as the basis of some brooding ruminations about our very identity as human beings.

    There is of course a long tradition of Anglo-American poets reimagining Greek myth for their own purposes. When Shelley used the figure of Prometheus in *Prometheus Unbound* (1820) as a symbol of human freedom from social and religious restraints, he was writing in the wake of the French Revolution and its overthrow of an absolutist monarchy and an autocratic and repressive Catholic church. In his afterword to *anOther Mythology*, Gold states that he uses Greek myth to highlight the status of "queers"—those who are non-hetero-normative—in our culture. It is a laudable goal, and Gold is generally successful in drawing upon those elements of myth that serve his purposes.

    But it would be too narrow to think that Gold is merely advocating a political agenda in these works. Throughout this slim booklet we can detect—and relish—his distinctive gifts in the use of language. Consider the first paragraph of "Below, the Pit":

> Below the skies, and farther still, haunting those bewildered spaces where tiny cracks formed at the fork of maybe-so, on the banks of trembling rivers at the base of unformed nightmares, I waited in the Pits cleaved from black and brittle sanguinity. A glass-blown geography of the horrid flames of yesterday glazed across a plain that once had woods but now held only deserts and mountains cut down into oceans of jagged diamonds and rocks bleeding into the bodies of five rivers.

The secret of this passage's effectiveness is Gold's deftness in choosing the unexpected word at exactly the right moment. At the end of that first sentence, "sanguinity" (i.e., bloodiness) is not at all what we expect, especially as we struggle to determine how bloodiness can be "black and brittle." But that is exactly what a prose poem should do: it shakes us out of our complacency—linguistic, philosophical, and sociocultural—by forcing us to envision new and disturbing thoughts and images. "Oceans of jagged diamonds" does the same thing; and the reference to "five rivers" evokes the five rivers of Hades, some of which—Acheron, Phlegethon, and Lethe—are cited in other prose poems in the book.

Much of Gold's work broaches the cosmic in an intense fashion. In "As Fate Would Have It," the sentence "Heat-death and chilled-chaos existed simultaneously in the universe, and there I was, floating in the middle of it all" melds cosmicism with existential angst in a powerful manner.

This booklet, graced with splendid cover art by the prolific Dan Sauer, provides only a foretaste of Gold's work. Other volumes are in the works, and they will cumulatively exhibit what a unique voice he has become in contemporary weird fiction and poetry.

# Notes on Contributors

**Dmitri Akers** is a poet of the weird from Adelaide, South Australia (Kaurna country). For him, the cadaverous rot of Python still fills the air at Delphi; the Musai, too, cannot help but see monsters beneath Parnassus. His poetry and prose have appeared in *Penumbra, So It Goes, Midnight Echo,* and *Spectral Realms,* while he has an essay and review in the *Undergraduate Library* and the *Modernist Review*.

**Manuel Arenas** resides in Phoenix, Arizona, where he writes his Gothic fantasies and dark ditties sheltered behind heavy curtains, as he shuns the oppressive orb that glares down on him from the cloudless, dust filled desert sky. His work has appeared in various genre publications, most notably in the poetry journal *Spectral Realms*.

**David Barker** has been writing supernatural fiction and poetry since the 1980s. His latest book is *12 Foot Skeleton Poems*. David's work has appeared in many magazines and anthologies, including *Fungi, Cyäegha, Weird Fiction Review, The Audient Void, Nightmare's Realm, Forbidden Knowledge, Spectral Realms, The Art Mephitic, A Walk in a Darker Wood, A Walk in a City of Shadows, For the Outsider: Poems Inspired by H. P. Lovecraft,* and *Weird Fiction Quarterly*.

**Leigh Blackmore** horror fiction has appeared in more than sixty magazines from *Avatar* to *Strange Detective Stories*. He has reviewed for journals including *Lovecraft Annual, Shoggoth, Skinned Alive,* and *Dead Reckonings*. His critical essays appear in volumes including Benjamin Szumskyj's *The Man Who Collected Psychos: Critical Essays on Robert Bloch,* Gary William Crawford's *Ramsey Campbell: Critical Essays on the Modern Master of Horror,* Danel Olson's *21st Century Gothic,* and elsewhere. New weird verse has appeared in *Penumbra* and other journals.

**Benjamin Blake** is the author of the novel *The Devil's Children* and the poetry collections *Standing on the Threshold of Madness, Southpaw Nights* (poetry and prose), *All the Feral Dogs of Los Angeles* (with Cole Bauer), *Dime Store Poetry*, and *Tenebrae in Aeternum* (published by Hippocampus Press).

**Adam Bolivar**, a native of Boston now residing in Portland, Oregon, published his weird fiction and poetry in the pages of *Nameless*, the *Lovecraft eZine*, *Spectral Realms*, and Chaosium's *Steampunk Cthulhu* and *Atomic Age Cthulhu* anthologies. Hippocampus Press published his collections *The Lay of Old Hex* in 2017 and *Ballads for the Witching Hour* in 2022.

**William Clunie** is an American poet living in Berlin. His work has appeared in *Dreams and Nightmares*, *Star\*Line*, and as a collection from Demain Publishing, *Laws of Discord*. He would like to think his primary influences are Shakespeare, Milton, and Poe. He is married to a German woman named Sandra. They are quite happy together.

**Frank Coffman** is a retired professor of college English, creative writing, and journalism. He has published speculative poetry and fiction in a variety of journals, magazines, and anthologies. His fourth large collection of speculative verse, *What the Night Brings*, was published in August 2023. A collection of his short fiction, *Maxime Miris: 15 Tales of the Weird, Horrific, and Supernatural*, will be out in early 2024. Writing formal poetry in the *Weird Tales* tradition is his mission.

**Scott J. Couturier** is a Rhysling Award–nominated poet and prose writer of the weird, liminal, and darkly fantastic. His work has appeared in numerous venues, including *The Audient Void*, *Spectral Realms*, *Tales from the Magician's Skull*, *Space and Time Magazine*, *Cosmic Horror Monthly*, and *Weirdbook*; his collection of weird fiction, *The Box*, is available from Hybrid Sequence Media, while his collection of autumnal & folk horror verse, *I Awaken In October*, is available from Jackanapes Press.

**Deborah L. Davitt** was raised in Nevada, but currently lives in Houston with her husband and son. Her award-winning poetry and prose has appeared in over seventy journals, including the *Magazine of Fantasy & Science Fiction*, *Asimov's*, *Analog*, and *Lightspeed*. Her poetry collections *The Gates of Never* and *Bounded by Eternity* were nominated for the Elgin Award.

**Kendall Evans's** stories and poems have appeared in nearly all the major science fiction and fantasy magazines, including *Asimov's, Analog, Weird Tales, Strange Horizons, Weirdbook, Mythic Delirium, Dreams & Nightmares, Space & Time, Nebula Award Showcase* (2012), *The Magazine of Speculative Poetry, Amazing Stories, Fantastic Stories,* and many others. He is the author of the novels *The Rings of Ganymede* and *The Adventures of Ching Shih, Pirate Princess.*

**Joshua Gage** is an ornery curmudgeon from Cleveland. He currently co-edits the horror poetry journal *Otoroshi Journal* with his life partner, Rowan Beckett. His newest chapbook, *blips on a screen*, is available on Cuttlefish Books. He is a graduate of the Low Residency MFA Program in Creative Writing at Naropa University. He has a penchant for Pendleton shirts, Ethiopian coffee, and any poem strong enough to yank the breath out of his lungs.

**Wade German**'s most recent full-length poetry collection is *Psalms and Sorceries* (Hippocampus Press, 2022). His first collection, *Dreams from a Black Nebula*, is also available from Hippocampus Press. Other titles include four slim volumes of his selected poems with Portuguese translation: *Incantations, Apparitions, Phantasmagorias,* and the latest, *Chapel of Celluloid* (Raphus Press, 2023).

**Maxwell I. Gold** is a Jewish-American multiple award-nominated author who writes prose poetry and short stories in cosmic horror and weird fiction with half a decade of writing experience. He is a five-time Rhysling Award nominee and two-time Pushcart Award nominee.

**Amelia Gorman** lives in Eureka, California, where she spends her free time exploring the tide pools and redwoods with her dogs and foster dogs. Her fiction has appeared in *Nightscript* 6 and *Cellar Door* from Dark Peninsula Press. You can read some of her recent poetry in *New Feathers, Vastarien,* and *Penumbric*. Her first chapbook, the Elgin Award–winning *Field Guide to Invasive Species of Minnesota*, is available from Interstellar Flight Press.

**Joshua Green** is an author of weird fiction, fantasy, and science fiction. His work has appeared or is forthcoming in *British Fantasy Society:*

*Horizons, Strange Aeon, Spectral Realms, Penumbra, Calliope Interactive,* and elsewhere. He has three wonderful children and a miniature Australian shepherd named Juni.

**Tylor James** resides in Sweet Hollow, Wisconsin, and is a writer of the weird and macabre. His books include *Matters Most Macabre, Beneath the Jack-O-Lantern Sky: Tales of Sweet Hollow,* and *Old Dark Houses: A Halloween Novel.* His tales have been published in *Cosmic Horror Monthly, Strange Horizons, Weird House Magazine,* and several anthologies. He is twenty-nine years old.

**Ron L. Johnson II** has received honorable mention from *Photographer's Forum* and has been published in the *Best of College Photography Annual* and *St. Charles Suburban Journal.* Since digitalization has put film on the endangered list, he writes now with words instead of light. He has also been published in previous issues of *Spectral Realms.* And Ron has an article on "The Dunwich Horror" and *Ghostbusters* in the 2023 issue of the *Lovecraft Annual.*

**Katherine Kerestman** is the author of *Lethal* (PsychoToxin Press, 2023) and *Creepy Cat's Macabre Travels* (WordCrafts Press, 2020), as well as the co-editor (with S. T. Joshi) of *The Weird Cat* (WordCrafts Press, 2023). Her Lovecraftian and Gothic works have been featured in *Black Wings VII, Penumbra, Journ-E, Illumen, Retro-Fan* and *The Little Book of Cursed Dolls* (Media Macabre, 2023), and elsewhere.

**David C. Kopaska-Merkel** won the 2006 Rhysling Award for best long poem (for a collaboration with Kendall Evans), and edits *Dreams & Nightmares* magazine (since 1986). He has edited *Star*Line* and several *Rhysling* anthologies. His poems have been published in *Asimov's, Analog, Strange Horizons,* and elsewhere. His latest collection, *Some Disassembly Required,* winner of the 2023 Elgin Award, was published by Diminuendo Press in 2022.

**Lori R. Lopez** is a quirky author, illustrator, poet, and songwriter who likes to wear hats. Her Gothic-toned and extensive poetry collection *Darkverse: The Shadow Hours* was nominated for the 2018 Elgin Award, while individual poems have been nominated for Rhysling Awards.

Stories and verse appear in numerous publications. Other titles include *The Dark Mister Snark, Leery Lane, Odds & Ends, The room at the end of the hall, Cryptic Consequences,* and *An Ill Wind Blows.*

Despite the damnably suggestive *hints* in the various reviews, essays, and short stories published under his name in the eighties and nineties, the disappearance of **Simon MacCulloch** as the millennium drew to a close aroused no concern. Even when, some two decades later, unmentionably eldritch rimes supposedly written by him began to seep miasmically into the nether reaches of the independent press, none foresaw the opening up of hideous vistas of reality that such a blasphemously unnatural resurgence implied.

**Kurt Newton**'s poetry has appeared in numerous magazines and anthologies. He is the author of eight collections of poetry. His ninth collection, *Songs of the Underland and Other Macabre Machinations,* was recently published by Ravens Quoth Press.

**Ngo Binh Anh Khoa** is a teacher of English in Ho Chi Minh City, Vietnam. In his free time, he enjoys daydreaming, reading, and occasionally writing poetry for personal entertainment. His speculative poems have appeared in NewMyths.com, *Heroic Fantasy Quarterly, The Audient Void,* and other venues.

**Manuel Pérez-Campos**'s poetry has appeared previously in *Spectral Realms* and *Weird Fiction Review*. A collection of his poetry in the key of the weird is in progress; so is a collection of ground-breaking essays on H. P. Lovecraft. He lives in Bayamón, Puerto Rico.

**Michael Potts** is the author of three novels: *End of Summer, Unpardonable Sin,* and *Obedience,* all published by WordCrafts Press. He also has published three volumes of poetry: *From Field to Thicket* (winner, 2006 Mary Belle Campbell Poetry Book Award, North Carolina Writers Network), *Hiding from the Reaper and Other Horror Poems,* and *Slipknot and Other Dark Poems.* He serves as Professor of Philosophy, Methodist University, Fayetteville, North Carolina.

**Carl E. Reed** is employed as the showroom manager for a window, siding, and door company just outside Chicago. Former jobs include U.S. marine, long-haul trucker, improvisational actor, cab driver, security guard, bus driver, door-to-door encyclopedia salesman, construction worker, and art show MC. His poetry has been published in the *Iconoclast* and *Spectral Realms*; short stories in *Black Gate* and *newWitch* magazines.

**Geoffrey Reiter** is Associate Professor and Coordinator of Literature at Lancaster Bible College. He is also an Associate Editor at the website *Christ and Pop Culture,* where he frequently writes about weird horror and dark fantasy. As a scholar of weird fiction, Reiter has published academic articles on such authors as Arthur Machen, Bram Stoker, Clark Ashton Smith, and William Peter Blatty. His poetry has previously appeared in *Spectral Realms* and *Star\*Line,* and his fiction has appeared in *Penumbra* and *The Mythic Circle.*

**Ann K. Schwader** lives and writes in Colorado. Her newest collection, Unquiet Stars, is now out from Weird House Press. Two of her earlier collections, *Wild Hunt of the Stars* (Sam's Dot, 2010) and *Dark Energies* (P'rea Press, 2015), were Bram Stoker Award Finalists. In 2018, she received the Science Fiction and Fantasy Poetry Association's Grand Master award. She is also a two-time Rhysling Award winner.

**Darrell Schweitzer** has been publishing weird or fantastic poetry for decades. Not counting comic verse (e.g., *They Never Found the Head: Poems of Sentiment and Reflection,* 2001) his two previous collections of (mostly weird) verse are *Groping Toward the Light* (2000) and *Ghosts of Past and Future* (2008). Hippocampus Press will soon issue a new volume, *Dancing Before Azathoth,* of previously uncollected and selected poems. His most recent story collection is *The Children of Chorazin* (Hippocampus, 2023) and his most recent anthology is *Shadows out of Time* (PS Publishing 2023).

**John Shirley** won the Bram Stoker Award for his book *Black Butterflies: A Flock on the Dark Side.* His first poetry collection, *The Voice of the Burning House,* has been nominated for the Elgin Award for poetry.

**Jay Sturner** is an award-winning poet, fiction writer, and naturalist from the Chicago suburbs. He is the author of several books of poetry and a collection of short stories. His writing has appeared in such publications as the *Magazine of Fantasy & Science Fiction*, *Space & Time*, *Not One of Us*, and *Star\*Line*, as well as previous issues of *Spectral Realms*.

**DJ Tyrer** is the person behind Atlantean Publishing and has been published in *The Rhysling Anthology*, issues of *Cyäegha*, *The Horrorzine*, *Scifaikuest*, *Sirens Call*, *Star\*Line*, *Tigershark*, and *The Yellow Zine*. The e-chapbook *One Vision* is available from Tigershark Publishing. *SuperTrump* and *A Wuhan Whodunnit* are available for download from Atlantean Publishing.

**Kyla Lee Ward** is a Sydney-based author, actor, and artist. Reviewers have accused her of being "gothic and esoteric," "weird and exhilarating," and of "giving me a nightmare." Her writing has garnered her Australian Shadows and Aurealis awards, she has placed in the Rhyslings and received multiple Stoker and Ditmar nominations. Her poetry is collected in *The Land of Bad Dreams* and *The Macabre Modern and Other Morbidities* from P'rea Press.

**Andrew White** is an aspiring writer who lives like a monk in the mountains of North Carolina. He is inspired by metal music, mythology, mysticism, and all things Gothic/Lovecraftian. Andrew loves nature, his family, and his books. He tries not to take himself too seriously.

**Steven Withrow** has written three chapbooks—*The Sun Ships*, *The Bedlam Philharmonic*, and *The Nothing Box*—and a collaborative collection, *The Exorcised Lyric* (with Frank Coffman). His speculative and dark fantasy poems have appeared in *Asimov's*, *Spectral Realms*, *Space & Time*, and *Dreams & Nightmares*. His work was nominated for the Rhysling and Elgin awards, and he wrote the libretto for a chamber opera based on a classic English ghost story. He lives on Cape Cod.

**Lee Clark Zumpe**, an entertainment editor with Tampa Bay Newspapers, earned his bachelor's degree in English at the University of South Florida. He began writing poetry and fiction in the early 1990s. His work has regularly appeared in a variety of literary journals and genre magazines over the last few decades.

# Index to *Spectral Realms* 11–20

Conspectus of issues:

11 = Summer 2019
12 = Winter 2020
13 = Summer 2020
14 = Winter 2021
15 = Summer 2021
16 = Winter 2022
17 = Summer 2022
18 = Winter 2023
19 = Summer 2023
20 = Winter 2024

*I. Index of Contributors*

Abourjeili, Carole  18.10–11, 80–81
Aiken, Conrad  15.122–26
Akers, Dmitri  18.102–3; 19.52–53; 20.49
Alexander, Samuel John  11.111–12
Allen, John Thomas  18.50–51, 95
Allen, Mike  12.28
Anderson, James Arthur  18.13
Anonymous  18.117–20
Arenas, Manuel  11.50–51, 104; 12.24–25, 76–77; 13.26, 79, 105; 14.19, 81; 15.38, 89, 117; 16.34–35, 82, 98–99; 17.54, 88–90; 18.93; 19.58
Arrington, Chelsea  11.16–17, 84–85; 12.58; 14.50–51
Balcom, Ross  11.34–35, 60–61; 12.41, 98; 13.53
Barker, David  11.11, 42, 94–95; 12.7, 59; 13.40; 14.52–53, 87; 15.33, 79, 109; 16.37; 17.27, 77; 18.49, 101; 19.19, 83; 20.34
Barlow, R. H.  13.115
Bergmann, F. J.  11.14, 102–3; 13.38, 99; 15.52–53, 94; 19.86–87

Blackmore, Leigh  12.26–27, 83; 13.41, 87; 14.26–27, 83; 15.134–36; 17.10–11; 18.125–29; 19.23; 20.31
Blake, Benjamin  12.30–31; 13.67; 16.43; 18.92; 19.26; 20.17
Boatman, Garrett  19.42–44
Bolivar, Adam  11.39, 74–75; 12.38–39; 14.56–57; 15.63–65, 112–14; 16.13, 83; 17.26, 66, 110–11; 18.46; 19.64; 20.35–42
Boylan, Kieran Dacey  12.23, 92–93
Breiding, G. Sutton  11.46–48
Brock, Sunni K  13.132–33
Calhoun, Pat  11.36
Clark, G. O.  11.22, 68–69; 14.58–59; 17.70
Clare, John  14.113–14
Clunie, William  18.62; 19.56–57; 20.74–77
Coffman, Frank  11.31; 12.32–34; 88; 13.22–24, 81, 92–93; 14.14–15, 67, 100–103; 15.23, 75–78, 96–97; 16.24, 62–65, 106–8; 17.21, 69; 18.9 18.55–56, 98–99;

19.12–13, 66–68, 94–96; 20.13, 60–63
Collingwood, Christopher 11.20–21, 76–77
Coolbrith, Ina 16.109
Couturier, Scott C. 11.32–33, 78–80; 12.14–15, 73–75, 94–95; 13.54–55, 90, 112–14; 14.22–23, 78–79, 98–99; 15.26–27, 86–88; 16.32–33, 58–59, 103; 17.24–25, 64–65, 108–9; 18.14–16, 60–61, 96; 19.9, 70, 90–91; 20.9, 28–30, 80–81
Coverley, Harris 14.43; 16.36, 80–81; 18.21, 64–66, 112–13
Curtis, Margaret 16.60–61, 17.94–95
Cushing, Nicole 12.49–51
Darwin, Erasmus 19.107–08
Davitt, Deborah L. 12.20–21, 85; 20.22, 73
Day, Holly 12.40; 16.75; 18.23, 73
Dickinson, Christian 18.12, 77, 111; 19.37, 92, 98
Dilks, Steve 18.32–34
Dioses, Ashley 11.54–55; 12.16; 13.63; 14.68; 15.116; 17.33; 18.78
Dompieri, Patricia 19.10–11
Donlon, Linn 17.42, 104–5
Dowson, Ernest 12.103
Dumars, Denise 16.15, 50–51, 89; 17.59, 106; 19.54–55
Evans, Kendall 20.68
Fraser, Rebecca 17.22
Futter, Ian 11.100–101; 13.8–10; 14.8–9; 17.52–53; 19.28–29, 80–82
Gage, Joshua 15.108; 18.38–40; 20.78
Gardner, Adele 12.42; 13.14; 13.88–89; 16.10–11, 100–101; 18.18–19
Garriock, Liam 11.26–27; 19.78–79

German, Wade 11.9, 57; 12.9, 44, 87; 13.30–32, 78, 103; 14.46, 82; 15.20–21, 68–70, 104–6; 16.23, 52, 102; 17.28–31, 68; 18.48, 91; 19.7; 20.51, 88–92
Goff, Thomas 14.48–49; 16.49; 17.63, 98–99
Gold, Maxwell I. 11.72–73; 12.13, 63, 99–100; 13.16–17, 68–69, 106–7; 14.24–25, 60–61, 97; 15.22, 66–67, 102–3; 16.14, 67, 96; 17.13, 107; 18.20, 94; 19.34, 69, 102; 20.8, 48, 87
Goodenough, Arthur 13.116–17
Góra, Norbert 11.40
Gorman, Amelia 18.42–44; 20.10–12
Grant, P. B. 15.71; 16.38, 88
Green, Joshua 19.39, 74; 20.23, 101
Gupta, Rahul 13.27–29, 82–83
Hardy, Jason/Jay 17.38–39, 62–63, 18.82–83
Hardy, Thomas 19.109–10
Hensley, Chad 12.36–37; 15.39; 17.81; 18.30–31
Hilton, Alicia 15.45–46, 72–73; 19.20–22, 88–89
Hopkins-Drewer, Cecelia 11.38; 12.48
Irving, Christine 16.28–29
James, Tylor 20.64–66
Jeffrey, Michelle 12.80–81
Johnson, Ron L., II 11.23, 67, 17.67; 18.57; 20.56
Johnson, Clay F. 14.40–42
Joshi, S. T. 12.107–10; 13.130–31; 14.119–23; 15.129–33; 19.113–16; 20.109–10
Kerestman, Katherine 18.130–32; 19.60–61; 20.26, 71
Khoa, Ngo Binh Anh 13.25, 70–74; 14.32–36, 69, 109; 15.7–13, 40–42, 107; 16.7, 53–55, 94; 17.18,

48-49, 96-97; 18.25, 68-72, 106-7; 19.36, 65, 99-100; 20.27, 20.72, 20.98-100
Kolarik, Andrew  18.108-9
Kopaska-Merkel, David C.  11.30, 63, 105-8; 13.39; 14.44-45; 17.46, 91-93; 18.54; 19.59; 20.84

Lafler, Henry Anderson  16.110-15
Landis, Geoffrey A.  11.44
Larson, Randall D.  11.43
Lawson, Curtis M.  11.49; 12.62
Legaria, Marcos  11.115-25; 17.125-30
Lopez, Lori R.  13.56-60; 14.16-18, 63-66, 94-95; 15.16-19, 57-61, 101; 16.18-20, 68-71; 17.14-17, 78-79; 18.27-29, 84-88; 19.14-17, 30-32; 20.52-55, 93
Lorraine, Lilith  17.119
LoSchiavo, LindaAnn  16.25, 78-79; 17.35, 87; 19.45
Lovecraft, Charles  13.43, 104; 14.88-90; 15.32, 81; 16.30, 74; 17.19, 55, 115-18

MacCulloch, Simon  20.50, 96
Mani, Mack W.  12.66-72; 16.40-42
Mare, Walter de la  14.115-16
Maybrook, Josh  12.22, 86; 13.15, 62; 14.86; 15.62; 17.103
Miller, Michael D.  12.54-55
Morton, James F.  18.121
Myers, D. L.  15.50-51; 18.47
Newton, Kurt  11.64-66; 16.76-77; 17.82-85; 20.24
Nightingale, C. d. G.  13.100-101

O'Melia, James  13.61; 18.104
Opperman, K. A.  11.37; 12.52; 13.47; 14.47; 15.15; 18.17, 90

Pérez-Campos, Manuel  11.15, 56, 86; 12.19, 35, 82; 13.11, 75, 102; 14.70, 80, 110-12; 15.47; 16.16-17, 84, 104-5; 17.36-37, 71, 112-13; 18.26, 67, 100; 19.38, 73, 104; 20.18-19, 20.57, 20.94-95
Permenter, Justin  15.98-100
Phillips, Fred  14.26-27
Pissantchev, Andrey  13.48-52
Potts, Michael  20.58
Reed, Carl E.  11.12-13, 41, 87-91; 12.12, 53, 96-97; 13.12-13, 86, 111; 14.20-21, 72-73, 106; 15.34-37, 85, 118-20; 16.8-9, 45-48, 97; 17.12, 47, 100-102; 18.7, 58-59, 105; 19.8, 46-47, 97; 20.14, 46-47, 86
Reiter, Geoffrey  14.7, 76-77, 107; 15.25, 54-55, 115; 16.27, 93; 17.43, 56-58; 18.22, 76, 114; 19.27; 20.59
Riddle, Silvatiicus  18.52-53; 19.84-85
Rozinski, Allan  11.58-59; 12.78-79; 13.64-66; 14.85

Sammons, David  12.56-57
Schembri, David  14.54-55; 17.50-51
Schwader, Ann K.  11.28-29, 81; 13.18, 91; 14.12-13, 96; 15.28, 16.21, 66; 18.36-37, 89; 19.25; 20.33
Schweitzer, Darrell  11.45; 12.17, 84; 13.33; 14.30-31, 92-93; 15.90; 16.31, 85; 17.23, 80; 18.45; 19.49; 20.32, 82-83
Sharp, William  20.105
Shaw, Mary C.  20.106
Shirley, John  16.39; 17.20; 20.7, 43
Sidney-Fryer, Donald  11.129-34; 12.111-13; 13.121-29; 14.124-29; 16.119-23, 123-28
Sinclair, May  11.109-10
Smith, Claire  11.92-93; 13.76-77; 14.38-39; 15.74; 16.26; 17.60-62; 19.76-77
Smith, Oliver  11.98-99; 12.45-47; 13.44-46; 14.84; 15.30-31, 82-83; 16.56-57; 17.72-74; 19.40-41

Snell, Bertrande Harry 17.120-21
Sng, Christina 11.24-25, 62, 96-97; 12.60-61, 89-91; 13.34-37; 14.10-11, 75, 14.104-5; 16.12, 90-92
Strange, Tatiana 11.18-19, 82-83; 13.19
Sturner, Jay 15.95; 16.86-87; 17.40-41; 19.50-51; 20.69-70
Symons, Arthur 12.104

Tennyson, Alfred, Lord 15.121
Terry, Ronald 13.20-21, 80
Tierney, Richard L. 13.7; 17.9
Tyrer, DJ 14.37, 71, 108; 15.43-44, 91; 16.22; 17.32, 75, 114; 18.79; 19.48, 93; 20.20-21
Tyrrell, Thomas 11.52-53; 12.10-11; 13.94-98

Ward, Kyla Lee 20.15, 79

Webb, Don 12.18; 17.45; 19.33
Webb, M. F. 11.71; 12.8; 15.14, 56; 18.8
White, Andrew 17.34, 76; 18.24, 63, 97; 19.18, 72; 20.25, 85
Wildes, Abigail 11.10; 15.80
Wilson, Andrew J. 12.43
Wilson, Mary Krawczak 11.70; 12.29; 13.42
Withrow, Steven 12.64-65; 13.84-85, 108-10; 14.28-29, 74, 91; 15.29, 84, 110-11; 16.72-73; 18.35, 74-75, 110, 132-34; 19.71, 35; 20.35-42

Zumpe, Lee Clark 19.24, 75, 103; 20.16, 67, 97
Zuniga, Jordan 14.62; 15.24, 48-49; 15.92-93; 16.44, 95; 17.44, 86; 18.41

*II. Index of Titles*

"Absence of Clouds, The" (Clark) 11.68-69
"Acid Rain" (Khoa) 16.7
"Acrostic Sonnet for Wilum Hopfrog Pugmire" (Barker) 12.7
"Aesthetic of Grotesquerie, An" (Blackmore) 15.134-36
"After an Industrial Accident" (Withrow) 18.74-75
"After Heathcliff Digs Up Cathy" (Potts) 20.58
"After Hesse" (Webb) 19.33
"After Verdun: A Psychomantic Vision" (Pérez-Campos) 13.11
"Alanna" (Boatman) 19.42-44
"All Fires Light the Wicker Man" (Couturier) 16.58-59
"All That I Have Lost" (Sng) 13.34-37
"Allure of the Western Sky" (Sturner) 15.95
"Altagracia's Lament" (Arenas) 16.34-35

"Altar of Yig" (Barker) 11.42
"American Omar, An" (Joshi) 19.113-16
"Among the Dead" (Couturier) 18.96
"Among the Petroglyphs" (Schwader) 13.18
"Amongst the Flowers" (Couturier) 14.98-99
"Amongst the Sargasso" (Couturier) 13.54-55
"Anathema" (Lopez) 20.52-55
"Ancient Rite: A Walk amongst the Corn" (Reed) 19.46-47
"Another Apocalypse" (Zumpe) 19.24
"Antiquarian Research" (Kopaska-Merkel) 17.46
"Apostate's Eschatology, An" (Reed) 19.97
"Appalling" (Lopez) 18.26-28
"Appeals of Arianwen, Recruiter of Monsters, The" (Reed) 14.20-21

"Arch Wizardry, the Glorious Opulence of St Toad" (Lovecraft) 14.88-90
"Arms of Death, The" (Clark) 14.58-59
"As One Poet to Another (Breiding) 11.46-48
"As the Dream Descends" (Newton) 16.76-77
"Aspis; or, The Brood of Rahab" (Coverley) 18.21
"Assailant from the Unknown" (Barker) 15.33
"Astral Parasites" (Pérez-Campos) 12.82
"Astray" (Bergmann) 13.38
"At the Polar Gatefires" (Kolarik) 18.108-09
"Aubade" (Grant) 16.88
"Ave, Hell's Angel!" (Reed) 14.72-73
"Baker at the Beggar's Wedding, The" (Gorman) 20.10-12
"Baleful Beldam, The" (Arenas) 11.104
"Ballade of the Plague Orgy of Moloch" (German) 15.20-21
"Banquet of Thalassa, The" (Smith) 15.30-31
"Banshee" (Dickinson) 18.12
"Bard of Grain and Gourd" (Opperman) 18.90
"Battle against the Dark Lord" (Zuniga) 17.44
"Battlefield, The" (Bolivar) 19.64
"Bayou, The" (Zumpe) 19.75
"Beast with a Billion Stomachs, The" (Gold) 16.67
"Beautiful Beast" (Smith) 15.74
"Bedlam Philharmonic, The" (Withrow) 12.64-65
"Beneath the Mirror Moon" (Khoa) 20.72
"Beneath the Ruins of Xul-Kizaak" (German) 18.91

"Beside the Dead" (Coolbrith) 16.109
"Betrayed" (Irving) 16.28-29
"Beyond the Fields" (Wilson) 12.43
"Biting Sarcasm" (Lopez) 14.63-66
"Black Goat, The" (Donlon) 17.42
"Black Hymeneal" (Arenas) 15.38
"Black-Tongue Kiss" (Reed) 11.87-91
"Black-Winged Battle Cry" (Reed) 15.118-20
"Black Wings Return" (Miller) 12.54-55
"Blackbird's Ghost, The" (Wildes) 11.10
"Blackburn's Bloom" (Arenas) 17.88-90
"Blindsight" (Lopez) 17.78-79
"Bog Man, The" (Arrington) 11.84-85
"Bog-Track, The" (Schwader) 16.21
"Bold Voyager" (Schweitzer) 17.80
"Bone Man, The" (Green) 20.23
"Bone or Root" (Dumars) 19.54-55
"Bone-Taster" (Goff) 16.49
"Boneless, The" (Blackmore) 19.23
"Bookshop on the Wharf, The" (Barker) 15.109
"Born under Saturn Indeed" (Sidney-Fryer) 16.119-23
"Bottled Dredge, A" (Lovecraft) 15.81
"Boy Meets Girl" (Kopaska-Merkel) 19.59
"Brain Funk" (Gold) 18.20
"Bridal Bower" (Barker) 14.87
"Bring Out Your Dead and Other Speculations" (Sidney-Fryer) 14.124-29
"Brocéliande" (Arenas) 19.58
"Burning Man, The" (Withrow) 14.91
"By Creator Forsaken" (Couturier) 20.80-81
"By the Sea" (Barker) 19.83

"By What Right Do You Call Yourself Patience?" (Goff) 17.63
"Cabin in the Wood, A" (Coffman) 19.66-68
"Caged Animals" (Withrow) 14.28-29
"Call of Lizzie, The" (Reed) 15.34-37
"Calling All Witches" (Gardner) 13.88-89
"Candy Corn Caresses" (Dioses) 17.33
"Carcoza" (Tyrer) 15.43-44
"Carrion Dreams" (Gold) 12.99-100
"Carrot and Stick" (Withrow) 15.84
"Cassandra Can't Tell You" (Rozinski) 11.58-59
"Cast" (Johnson) 17.67
"Casting Out: A Failure, A" (Blake) 20.17
"Castle Beneath the Hedgerow, The" (Riddle) 19.84-85
"Catacombs, The" (Strange) 13.19
"Cats Which Walk in Dreams" (Donlon) 17.104-5
"Cetus" (German) 14.82
"Chants of Moros, The" (German) 14.46
"Children of the Night" (Tyrer) 16.22
"Christmas Lure" (Hilton) 19.88-89
"Churchyard Passacaglia" (Goff) 17.98-99
"Cicada Kings, The" (Green) 19.39
"City of Carrion, Valley of Darkness" (Coverley) 16.80-81
"City of Dreams" (Gold) 16.96
"City of Skulls" (Gold) 13.16-17
"Clark Ashton Smith and Robert Nelson: Master and Apprentice (Part 3)" (Legaria) 11.115-25
"Clingers, The" (Coffman) 16.24
"Close Behind" (Coffman) 15.23
"Cometfall" (Tyrer) 17.32

"Communion" (Pérez-Campos) 17.36-37
"confession" (Zumpe) 19.103
"Conjuring, The" (Coffman) 12.88
"Conspiracy Penetrated, A" (Reed) 13.86
"Corvid Hill" (Barker) 18.49
"Costume, The" (Lopez) 15.57-61
"Countess, The" (Allen) 18.95
"Court of Azathoth, The" (Khoa) 17.48-49
"Covert" (Bergmann) 11.14
"Creature of the Twilight, A" (German) 17.28-31
"Crime of Passion, A" (Clark) 17.70
"Crimson Knight, The" (Couturier) 12.14-15
"Crow Is Calling, A" (Lopez) 15.101
"Cruel Eleanora" (Bolivar) 11.74-75
"Crypt Currency" (German) 16.102
"Daemon Lord, The" (Hensley) 17.81
"Daemon Masque, The" (Bolivar) 15.112-14
"Damned: A Ghazal, The" (Gage) 15.108
"Dancing Before Azathoth" (Schweitzer) 14.92-93
"Dark Axiom" (Pérez-Campos) 20.18-19
"Dark Château, The" (Mare) 14.115-16
"Dark Descent, The" (Khoa) 14.109
"Dark Oracles Indeed" (Sidney-Fryer) 12.111-13
"Dark Sister" (Zumpe) 20.97
"Dark Sorcerer, The" (Lovecraft) 16.74
"dark wishes" (Zumpe) 20.16
"Darkest Days and Nights, The" (Blake) 19.26
"Date Night" (Elmes) 16.15
"Daughters of Phorcys" (German) 20.88-92

"De Quincey Mutations: Our Ladies of Sorrow" (German) 13.30–32
"Dearg-Due An Irish Legend of Horror, The" (Coffman) 14.100–103
"Death Confession: A Golden Shovel" (LoSchiavo) 17.35
"Death of the Sculptor's Model, The" (Withrow) 19.71
"Death's Kingdom" (Zuniga) 15.48–49
"Demon Ball, The" (Strange) 11.82–83
"Demonic and Darkling" (Blackmore) 18.125–29
"Deserted House, The" (Tennyson) 15.121
"Destiny" (Schembri) 17.50–51
"Digging Beneath the Battlefield" (Withrow) 16.72–73
"Diner of Delights" (Smith) 11.92–93
"Dionysus in San Rafael" (Goff) 14.48–49
"Disclosure" (Góra) 11.40
"Display of Affection, A" (Coverley) 18.112–13
"Divided by Demons" (Wilson) 11.70
"Djinn" (Dickinson) 18.77
"Doctor Fulci's Fantastic Cure for Nightmares" (Garriock) 11.26–27
"Dominion of the Son of the Dragon, The" (Zuniga) 16.95
"Dominion of the Wicked, The" (Zuniga) 14.62
"Doom, The" (Reiter) 20.59
"Doubled Word" (Gupta) 13.27–29
"Down the Garden Path" (Webb) 11.71
"Dr. Ripper, I Presume?" (Reed) 13.111
"Dragon's Rage, The" (Khoa) 18.68–72
"Draining Chair, The" (Tyrrell) 13.94–98

"Dream, A" (Sharp) 20.105
"Dream Hackers" (Gold) 12.63
"Dream Snatchers" (Khoa) 13.25
"Dreams of the Styx" (Dilks) 18.32–34
"Dreamsign" (White) 18.24
"Duke of Balladry, The" (Bolivar) 11.39
"Dusk" (White) 17.76
"Ealren Halgena Æfen" (German) 16.52
"Echoing Dylan Thomas; or, A Cri de Coeur from Reader to Writer" (Reed) 20.46–47
"*Eden* Spills, The" (Grant) 15.71
"Egyptian Splendor, The" (Balcom) 12.98
"Eidolon Tetratych" (Coffman) 16.62–65
"Elizabeth Siddal Rossetti, Cemetery Superstar" (LoSchiavo) 17.87
"Empty House, The" (Maybrook) 14.86
"End of Day, The" (Khoa) 19.65
"Epiphany on the Bronze Poseidon at Cape Sounion" (Pérez-Campos) 19.73
"Epiphany" (Webb) 15.14
"Essential Guide to the Land of Dream" (Kopaska-Merkel) 17.91–93
"Eternal Lovers" (Reed) 11.12–13
"Eternal Night" (Reiter) 14.107
"Eye of Sapphire, Eye of Emerald" (Newton) 17.82–85

"Face Your Future" (Tyrer) 19.48
"Fairies from the Twilight Forest" (Sng) 14.104–05
"Fairiest, The" (Smith) 11.98–99
"Fairy Rings, The" (Clare) 14.113–14
"Fat Man and Yellow-Eyes: A Ghoulish Tale" (Reed) 17.100–102
"Fatal Attraction" (Khoa) 15.107

"Father's Bullet: A Tale of the Apocalypse" (Reed) 16.8–9
"Faust Unrepentant" (Maybrook) 15.62
"Fée Metropolitain" (Webb) 18.8
"Ferryman's Rest, The" (Green) 19.74
"Figments and Fragments" (Clunie) 18.62
"Final Conquest, The" (Khoa) 15.40–42
"Final Night" (Tyrer) 18.79
"Final Scrawl, The" (Calhoun) 11.36
"Flotsam of Want, The" (Smith) 16.26
"Flower of Evil" (Arenas) 17.54
"Fog" (Shaw) 20.106
"Footsteps in the Night" (Khoa) 17.18
"For an Autumn Willow" (Couturier) 20.9
"For Those Who Tread the Narrow Path" (Zuniga) 18.41
"Frankenskin for Frankenbones" (Smith) 19.40–41
"Fright" (Sinclair) 11.109–10
"From Heights of Fire to Depths of Cold" (White) 18.63
"Front Piece from the *Necronomicon*" (Anderson) 18.13
"Frosty Love" (Lovecraft) 16.30
"Frozen Voices" (Blackmore) 13.87
"Fuath" (Dickinson) 18.111
"Funeral of a Vampire" (Lorraine) 17.119

"Gaia's Prophecy" (Shirley) 20.43
"Galactic Cellars, Unhinged" (Gold) 14.97
"Garden of Night, The" (White) 17.34
"Gata, La" (Lopez) 17.14–17
"Gathering, The" (Webb) 15.56
"Genesis" (Day) 12.40

"Genevieve and Amun" (Hilton) 19.20–22
"Ghebulax" (Gold) 12.13
"Ghost Factory, The" (Bergmann) 11.102–3
"Ghostly Shade of Oil, A" (Smith) 14.84
"Ghosts in Their Sunday Clothes" (Withrow) 18.35
"Ghosts' Autumnal Fair, The" (Khoa) 17.96–97
"Ghoul's Delirium, The" (Couturier) 18.14–16
"Giants in the Earth" (Schweitzer) 18.45
"Gilgamesh in Mourning" (Reiter) 16.93
"Goblin Laughter" (German) 15.68–70
"God of Dark Fantasy Prose-Poetry, The" (Sturner) 16.86–87
"God of Phlegm, The" (Gold) 11.72–73
"God of the Winds, The" (Sng) 12.60–61
"Gods of the Garden" (Withrow) 19.35
"Golden Age, The" (Lovecraft) 17.19
"Golgotha of Horror, A" (Joshi) 12.107–10
"Gorgon Queen, The" (Johnson) 20.56
"Grave Vision, A" (Couturier) 19.9
"Grave-Robbing 2.0: Intermediate" (Schweitzer) 20.82–83
"Graves, The" (Withrow) 13.84–85
"Graveside Ghost" (Wilson) 12.29
"Graveyard of the Gods" (Couturier) 11.78–80
"Gray" (Webb) 12.8
"Gray Grimalkin" (Couturier) 16.32–33
"Great and Final Feast, The" (Sturner) 20.69–70

"Great Parade, The" (Gold) 16.14
"Great Wheel, The" (Coffman) 11.31
"Greetings from Krampus" (Arenas) 14.81
"Grindevil" (Lopez) 18.84–88
"Guidebook for Witches and Warlocks, A" (Sidney-Fryer) 11.129–34
"Guillotined" (Reed) 11.41
"H.P.L.: R.I.P." (Arenas) 14.19
"Haematophagy" (Dioses) 12.16
"Hand of Glory" (Arenas) 16.82
"Haruspex" (Landis) 11.44
"Harvest Reaped and Threshed, The" (Smith) 16.56–57
"Harvester, The" (Opperman) 13.47
"Haunted" (Terry) 13.80
"Haunted Houses" (Morton) 18.121
"Haunter, The" (Hardy) 19.109–10
"Haunter of College Hill, The" (Barker) 15.79
"He Who Waits" (Coffman) 13.81
"Hell-Flower" (Arenas) 13.79
"Heolstor" (Bolivar) 17.66
"Herod Agrippa" (German) 18.48
"Hic Aqua Est" (Gage) 20.78
"Hidebehind: A Legend of the North Country, The" (Coffman) 13.22–24
"Hill of Bones, The" (Clark) 11.22
"His Dark Light Shines" (Rozinski) 14.85
"Hollow Heart, A" (Davitt) 20.22
"Homage to *Creepy*" (Pérez-Campos) 12.19
"Homer Before the Trojan Court" (Schweitzer) 12.84
"Hounds of the Lord" (Permenter) 15.98–100
"House" (Fraser) 17.22
"House (A Conduit), The" (Mani) 12.66–72
"How Love Fled" (MacCulloch) 20.50
"How the World Ends" (Elmes) 17.106
"I Am Beautiful" (Dioses) 18.78
"I Awaken in October" (Couturier) 15.26–27
"I Met a Girl in a Cemetery" (Shirley) 17.20
"I See Too Much: A Clairvoyant's Complaint" (Coffman) 17.21
"I Want to Taste October" (Balcom) 12.41
"I'll Return in Late October" (Opperman) 12.52
"Iason's Prospicience; or, Solstyce" (Pérez-Campos) 18.100
"Igerna, Alone in Waning Moonlight" (Reiter) 14.76–77
"Ill Wind, An" (Barker) 14.52–53
"Illumination" (Barker) 18.101
"Illusion of Light" (Terry) 13.20–21
"Imaginary Friend" (Khoa) 13.70–74
"Imperishable" (Kopaska-Merkel) 13.39
"In a Breton Cemetery" (Dowson) 12.103
"In a Haunted Holler" (Bolivar) 16.83
"In Arcadia" (Maybrook) 12.86
"In Her Defence" (Smith) 17.60–62
"In Lakewood Cemetery" (James) 20.64–66
"In Medusa's Coils" (Tyrer) 19.93
"In the Beginning" (Elmes) 17.59
"In the Black Hours" (Schwader) 14.12–13
"In the Court of the Dragon" (Tyrer) 15.91
"In the Days of the Vertical Ocean" (Kopaska-Merkel) 11.63
"In the Forest, Where Wild Things Live" (Smith) 13.76–77
"In the Graveyard, Decomposing" (LoSchiavo) 16.25
"In the Land of Magma, Salt, and Glacier" (Gorman) 18.42–44

"In the Ruins" (Reiter) 18.114
"In the Small Hours (moon version)" (Hensley) 15.39
"In Tura" (Couturier) 18.60-61
"In Vino Veritas" (Kopaska-Merkel) 14.44-45
"In Your Dreams" (Riddle) 18.52-53
"Incubus" (Couturier) 17.64-65
"Incubus" (Grant) 16.38
"Infernal Carnival" (Khoa) 16.53-55
"Infernal Nocturne" (Khoa) 20.98-100
"Inquiry Regarding the Dead" (Barker) 11.94-95
"Interrupted" (Lopez) 19.14-17
"Into the Mouth of the Sea" (Gold) 20.8
"Invitation, An" (Smith) 19.76-77
"Iron-Sceptred Skeleton" (Akers) 19.52-53
"It Will Be Thus" (Goodenough) 13.116-17
"Ithaca, Finally" (Schweitzer) 13.33
"Jack Bloodybones" (Bolivar) 14.56-57
"Jack in Xanadu" (Bolivar) 12.38-39
"Jack-o'-Lantern Hearted, The" (Opperman) 11.37
"Jack Thunder" (Bolivar) 15.63-65
"Jenkin" (Balcom) 13.53
"King in Yellow, The" (Khoa) 16.94
"King of Cats, The" (Bolivar) 16.13
"King Pest" (Tierney) 13.7
"Kiss of Life" (Arenas) 12.76-77
"Knowing the Dragon" (Reiter) 17.43
"Lady and Her Monster, A" (Collingwood) 11.20-21
"Lady in the Wood, The" (Reiter) 17.56-58
"Lair of the Bat People" (Balcom) 11.60-61

"Language of Night" (Clunie) 19.56-57
"Lantern of September, The" (Couturier) 19.90-91
"Last Days of the Flu, The" (Day) 18.73
"Last Golem, The" (Rozinski) 12.78-79
"Last House, The" (Hardy) 19.62-63
"Last Refuge, The" (O'Melia) 18.104
"Last Soldier on the Beach" (Sturner) 17.40-41
"Laughter out of the Sea" (Gold) 15.102-03
"Lawrence Talbot" (Coffman) 14.67
"Legend of Vlad and Juztina, The" (Strange) 11.18-19
"Legion" (Blake) 13.67
"Lenore to Her Tragic Muse, Edgar Allan Poe" (Gardner) 16.10-11
"Lepidoptera, My Sweet" (Myers) 15.50-51
"Let There Be Light" (Reed) 18.105
"Lines on Austin Osman Spare's 'Arbor Vitae'" (Campos) 13.75
"Lines on the Mistress of an Old Sea-Town" (Pérez-Campos) 16.84
"Lines Written in a Providence Churchyard" (Barker) 12.59
"Little Song of Death, A" (Reed) 17.47
"Lob" (Coffman) 19.94-96
"Locus Horroris" (Coffman) 18.98-99
"Lord and Lady" (White) 20.25
"Lord Death" (Dioses) 13.63
"Lord of Dreaming" (Couturier) 14.78-79
"Lorelei, The" (Coffman) 16.106-8
"Love Came upon a Darkling Night" (Clunie) 20.74-77
"Love Song of the Lugubrious Gondolier" (Arenas) 18.93

"Loyal Companion" (Withrow) 18.110
"Lunar Mission" (Kerestman) 20.71
"Lycanthropic Howl" (Reed") 14.106
"Machine, The" (Futter) 19.80–82
"Mad Scientist's Assistant, The" (Schweitzer) 16.31
"Madhouse Getaway" (Pérez-Campos) 12.35
"Mail-Order Bride" (Hilton) 15.45–46
"Malice Must Dwell within Your Heart" (Schweitzer) 17.23
"Malvolio's Revenge" (Ward) 20.79
"Man of Gold" (Tyrer) 14.37
"Man with One Head, The" (Lopez) 14.16–18
"Manurog" (Arenas) 15.117
"Marble Fang" (Blake) 18.92
"March, The" (Khoa) 20.27
"Märchen (Fairy Tales)" (Reed) 13.12–13
"Matron, The" (Khoa) 19.99–100
"Meadows of Night, The" (Bergmann) 15.52–53
"Means of Summoning, A" (Withrow) 14.74
"Medusa" (Sng) 16.12
"Melinoë" (German) 13.78
"Memento Mori" (Shirley) 20.7
"Memories of Another Country" (Pérez-Campos) 14.110–12
"Methuselah" (German) 11.57
"Mimics, The" (Sng) 16.90–92
"Minoan Messages" (Coffman) 12.32–34
"Miranda's Resolve" (Ward) 20.15
"Miscreation of Life, A" (Johnson) 14.40–42
"Monsters of the Moor, The" (Coffman) 20.60–63
"Monsters Within, The" (Sng) 11.24–25
"Monstrous Word Is 'Man,' The" (Reed) 19.8

"Moon Is Made of Cat, The" (Kerestman) 20.26
"Moonfog" (German) 20.51
"Moonlit Waters" (Dioses) 15.116
"Moribond" (Arenas) 13.105
"Mortality's Metronome" (LoSchiavo) 19.45
"Mother Dearest" (Khoa) 15.7–13
"Mother of All Things" (Sng) 14.75
"Mother of Our Fate" (Tyrer) 20.20–21
"Mr. Illusive" (Coffman) 18.55–56
"Mukkelevi" (Elmes) 16.50–51
"My Bantam Black Fay" (Arenas) 13.26
"My Loveliest Manticore; or, The Queen of the Lamiae" (German) 12.87
"My Sweetheart's Name Is Despair" (Shirley) 16.39
"Mycophilia" (Tyrer) 14.71
"Myth of Nothing, The" (Gold) 19.34
"Mythology and Cosmicism" (Joshi) 20.109–10
"Nachzehrer, The" (Couturier) 17.24–25
"Nativity" (Barker) 17.77
"Necromancer's Charm, The" (Couturier) 11.32–33
"Necronomicon" (Maybrook) 12.22
"Necropolis" (Newton) 20.24
"Nevermore" (Gardner) 13.14
"Night Comes to Sesqua Valley" (Myers) 18.47
"Night of Mirth and Magic, The" (White) 20.85
"Night of the Dove" (Barker) 20.34
"Nightmare, The" (Darwin) 19.107–8
"Nightmare, The" (Reiter) 19.27
"Nightmares of Ink, Dreams in Blood" (Gold) 14.60–61
"No Happily-Ever-After" (Kerestman) 18.130–31

"No One Is Safe" (Blake) 12.30-31
"Nordic Instinct" (Lovecraft) 17.55
"North of Arkham" (Barker) 19.19
"Not All of Them Are Ghosts" (Schweitzer) 12.17
"Notre Dame Is Burning!" (Lopez) 13.56-60
"Novembering" (Schwader) 19.25
"Now and Forever" (Boylan) 12.92-93
"Nuckelavee" (Dickinson) 19.92
"O Iranon" (Lovecraft) 13.43
"October Is Coming" (Opperman) 15.15
"October's Law of Diminishing Returns" (Withrow) 18.132-34
"Ode to the Great God Pan" (Reed) 12.12
"Odysseus May Have Been a Scoundrel" (Schweitzer) 14.30-31
"Of Masks and Monsters" (Gold) 15.66-67
"Of Shapeshifters Spawned by the Revolution" (Pérez-Campos) 20.94-95
"Of the Swordsman of Words and Worlds: Eldritchard" (Lovecraft) 17.115-18
"Old Bone in the Bluebells, An" (Smith) 15.82-83
"Old Ones: A Ghazal, The" (Gage) 18.38-40
"Old Sorcery" (German) 15.104-6
"Oleander and Wolfsbane" (Hilton) 15.72-73
"On a Threadbare Photograph of H.P.L. at 66 College St." (Pérez-Campos) 11.15
"On an Autumnal Graveyard" (Couturier) 19.70
"On Finding the Man" (Day) 16.75
"On Gustave Moreau's Canvas The Apparition" (Pérez-Campos) 11.86
"On Reading Poe" (Maybrook) 17.103

"On the Fantasque Ballet Premiere of Afternoon of a Faun" (Pérez-Campos) 17.71
"On the Invitation, an Anonymous Oil Seen in a Flea Market" (Pérez-Campos) 19.38
"Otherworld" (Lopez) 16.18-20
"Our Ghosts Are Going Away" (Schweitzer) 15.90
"Our Lady of the Acherontia" (Rozinski) 13.64-66
"Our Last Halloween" (Gardner) 16.100-01
"Ouroboros" (Coffman) 13.92-93
"Outsider, The" (Reed) 16.97
"Pack The" (Couturier) 12.73-75
"Painting the Pandemic" (Futter) 14.8-9
"Palazzo San Felice" (Blake) 16.43
"Passive Vampire, The" (German) 13.103
"Path of Grey, The" (Bolivar) 17.26
"Pearl, The" (Lafler) 16.110-15
"Perfect World" (Schwader) 18.89
"Pericula Noctis" (Coffman) 18.9
"Permian-Triassic" (Reiter) 15.25
"Phantasmascope" (Sidney-Fryer) 16.123-28
"Phantasms" (German) 17.68
"Philosophy & Aesthetics of Horror, The" (Reed) 12.53
"Phoenix, The" (Khoa) 19.36
"Pilgrim in the Mist" (German) 12.9
"Pillarist of Leptis Magna, The" (Pérez-Campos) 16.16-17
"Pixie-Ring, The" (Couturier) 16.103
"Plague" (Lopez) 15.16-19
"Plague Maiden's Footprints, The" (Smith) 14.38-39
"Plague Queen's Song, The" (Cushing) 12.49-51
"Plague's Wake" (Dioses) 11.54-55
"Planet Fetish" (Hensley) 12.36-37
"Plaything" (Pérez-Campos) 15.47

"Poe, on the Morning After" (Webb) 12.18

"Poe" (Larson) 11.43

"Poltergeists of Park Slope, The" (LoSchiavo) 16.78-79

"Pontianak" (Dickinson) 19.37

"Pores of Earth, The" (Lovecraft) 13.104

"Post-anthropy" (Kopaska-Merkel) 18.54

"Postmortem" (Khoa) 18.25

"Primal Night" (Schwader) 20.33

"Printz's Oratory" (Withrow) 15.110-11

"Proem to the Fortress Unvanquishable" (Tyrrell) 12.10-11

"Promise for Today, A" (Gold) 17.13

"Protector, The" (Futter) 13.8-10

"Psychopomp, The" (Hopkins-Drewer) 12.48

"Pumpkin Ale" (Opperman) 18.17

"Queen of Dark Poetry, A" (Brock) 13.132-33

"R. H. Barlow and the Activist Poets: How Did They Meet?" (Legaria) 17.125-30

"Ravensong" (Lopez) 20.93

"Reading by Ghost Light" (Akers) 20.49

"Reading the Leaves" (Schwader) 15.28

"Red Land, Black Pharaoh" (Schwader) 13.91

"Red Tresses" (Couturier) 13.112-14

"Remains" (Kopaska-Merkel) 11.105-8

"Remains, The" (Dompieri) 19.10-11

"Reparation" (Sng) 11.62

"Retrieval" (Bergmann) 13.99

"Rider of the Pegasi, The" (Nightingale) 13.100-01

"Rite of Exploration, The" (Day) 18.23

"River Dweller" (Zuniga) 16.44

"Role of Monster I Embrace, The" (White) 18.97

"Rollin' Bone and Beaten Stones" (Coverley) 18.64-66

"Runestone" (Schwader) 14.96

"Runic Sword, The" (Blackmore) 14.26-27

"Sacred" (Zumpe) 20.67

"Safe" (Sng) 14.10-11

"Saith the Witch" (German) 16.23

"Salute to Robert E. Howard: A Texas Writer" (Reed) 20.14

"Sanctuary" (Wilson) 13.42

"Satanic Sonata" (Arenas) 12.24-25

"Savage Fantasies of Mr. Arbuthnot, The" (Pérez-Campos) 20.57

"Sea Dream" (MacCulloch) 20.96

"Séance, The" (Khoa) 18.106-7

"Secret Pool, The" (Schweitzer) 11.45

"Seeker's Lament, The" (Coffman) 17.69

"Seer Light" (Garriock) 19.78-79

"Semblance" (Barker) 17.27

"Separation, The" (Futter) 11.100-101

"Serenade for Black Plague Gwynneth" (Pérez-Campos) 16.104-5

"Shadow and Fire" (Schembri) 14.54-55

"'Shadows, You Say'" (Coffman) 15.96-97

"Shadowlands" (Blackmore) 14.83

"She Tasted of Gin and Death" (Lawson) 11.49

"Shoggoths" (Blackmore) 20.31

"Shuffling Horror" (Reed) 15.85

"Silent House, The" (Alexander) 11.111-12

"Silent Silver Sea, The" (Blackmore) 12.83

"Singularity" (Lawson) 12.62

"Siren, The" (Abourjeili) 18.10–11
"Sisters" (Arrington) 14.50–51
"Sisyphus Looks Up" (Reiter) 18.22
"Skeleton Dance: A Ballad, The" (Anonymous) 18.117–20
"Skeleton Dance, The" (Green) 20.101
"Sleep of Reason Produces Monsters: An Extended Surveil, The" (Reed) 17.12
"Sleeper, The" (Maybrook) 13.15
"Slouching toward Yuggoth" (Tierney) 17.9
"Slow the Night Grows Darker" (Sammons) 12.56–57
"Small Doses" (Bergmann) 19.86–87
"Solving for X" (Schwader) 11.81
"Some Books Are Forbidden for Good Reason" (Schweitzer) 20.32
"Song of Calamity Joe, The" (Pissantchev) 13.48–52
"Song of the Sword, The" (Bolivar) 18.46
"Song of Two Deaths, A" (Futter) 17.52–53
"Sorcerer in His Tower Contemplating Possible Success, The" (Schweitzer) 19.49
"Southern Gothic; or, Hillbilly Horror" (Reed) 12.96–97
"Space-Time" (Johnson) 11.23
"Sphinx" (Dickinson) 19.98
"Spider" (Webb) 17.45
"Spirit Mirror of Doctor Dee, The" (Schwader) 18.36–37
"Spleen (III)" (Tyrer) 14.108
"Splenetic IV: After Baudelaire" (Gupta) 13.82–83
"Squire of Sweven, The" (Bolivar) 17.110–11
"Star Dust" (Reiter) 16.27
"Starfall" (Elmes) 16.89

"Star-Treader: Emperor of Dreams, The" (Reed) 18.7
"Stela of Selos" (Couturier) 12.94–95
"Stranded in Mississippi" (Hensley) 18.30–31
"Strange Door, Odd Key" (Coffman) 19.12–13
"Strife" (Barlow) 13.115
"Styx" (Sng) 11.96–97
"Subterranean Hungers" (Kopaska-Merkel) 11.30
"Summoning of Demons, A" (Jeffrey) 12.80–81
"Sun Sings Loud and Clear, The" (Sidney-Fryer) 13.121–29
"Super-Position" (Johnson) 11.67
"Survive against the Swarm" (Zuniga) 17.86
"Surviving Samhain" (White) 19.18
"Swamp Maiden, The" (Zuniga) 15.24
"Sweet Discordia Lee" (Smith) 13.44–46
"Sweet Dreams of the Dead, The" (O'Melia) 13.61
"Sycophant of the Siren" (Sturner) 19.50–51
"Sympathy for Laocoön and His Sons" (Pérez-Campos) 19,104
"Tasty Treat, A" (Gardner) 12.42
"Tatterjack; or, The Murder of Mother Goose" (Bolivar-Withrow) 20.35–42
"Tears of Cerberus, The" (German) 12.44
"Tears of the Raven" (Collingwood) 11.76–77
"Télos: The Anxiety of Choice" (Gold) 15.22
"Telos Falling" (Gold) 20.87
"Temple of the Condor" (Schwader) 11.28–29
"Temptation Entombed" (Barker) 11.11
"Tenebrae" (German) 19.7

"Termination Shock" (Reiter) 15.54-55
"Terror and Poignancy" (Joshi) 13.130-31
"Testament of Doom: A Paean to Clark Ashton Smith" (Pérez-Campos) 13.102
"That Was Epic" (Gold) 20.48
"There upon the Threshold" (Reed) 20.86
"There's a Hole in the Sky" (Gold) 18.94
"They're Coming" (Gold) 19.69
"Thing That Watches While I Write, The" (Tyrrell) 11.52-53
"Those That We Meet in Dark Country Lanes" (Schweitzer) 16.85
"Those Who Rise from Orange Slime" (Opperman) 14.47
"Three Poets, Three Visions" (Joshi) 14.119-23
"Time of Day" (Hardy) 18.82-83
"Time's Vulture" (Blackmore) 12.26-27
"To a Cat-Daemon: A Litany of Antient Ægypt" (Pérez-Campos) 11.56
"To Gaelle Lacroix, Lone Survivor of the Trufort Massacre" (Withrow) 13.108-10
"To Hypnos, Refuter of My Ego" (Pérez-Campos) 14.70
"To Kiss Death's Shroud" (Couturier) 15.86-88
"To Richard L. Tierney: In Memoriam" (Blackmore) 17.10-11
"To the Wolves" (Couturier) 13.90
"Tomb of Wilum Hopfrog Pugmire, The" (German) 11.9
"Tomb without Walls" (Balcom) 11.34-35
"Tongueless Dead, The" (Blackmore) 13.41

"Tonight's Tale: Devil County, USA" (Mani) 16.40-42
"Torment of Flame, The" (Davitt) 20.73
"Towers, The" (Gold) 19.102
"Transmogrification" (Pérez-Campos) 18.26
"Transubstantiator of the Finite" (Pérez-Campos) 14.80
"Trapped in the Spiral Maze" (Gardner) 18.18-19
"Traveler, The" (Futter) 19.28-29
"Tremulous Expectancy" (Lovecraft) 15.32
"Troublemaker; or, To Escape Days of Idleness, The" (Pérez-Campos) 18.67
"Tryst, The" (Coffman) 20.13
"Twisted Grin" (Dioses) 14.68
"Two Contemporaries, One Classic" (Joshi) 15.129-33
"Two Haiku" (Coverley) 14.43
"Under a Sun Long-Estranged" (Couturier) 14.22-23
"Underwater Circus, The" (Newton) 11.64-66
"Ungodly Thing, An" (Zuniga) 15.92-93
"Unknown, The" (Lopez) 14.94-95
"Unlocking, The" (Barker) 16.37
"Unrepaired" (Tyrer) 17.114
"Urban Renewal" (Allen) 12.28
"Uses of Enchantment" (Bergmann) 15.94

"vampire dragon: a haiku" (Evans) 20.68
"Vampire" (Abourjeili) 18.80-81
"Vampire" (Snell) 17.120-21
"Vampire, The" (Symons) 12.104
"Vampire: 1914, The" (Aiken) 15.122-26
"Vampire-Need, The" (Hopkins-Drewer) 11.38
"Vampire Vigil" (Arenas) 11.50-51
"Variant, The" (Gold) 13.106-07

"Venomous Violins, The" (Johnson) 18.57

"Verses inspired by Le Horla" (Couturier) 20.28-30

"Villa Infestada, La" (Coffman) 15.75-78

"Vision, The" (Khoa) 14.69

"Vision of Carcosa, A" (Kopaska-Merkel) 20.84

"Visiting Hours" (Allen) 18.50-51

"Voice in the Night, A" (Reiter) 18.76

"Watch and Wait" (Curtis) 17.94-95

"Water Slave" (Coverley) 16.36

"We Met in No-Man's-Land" (Reed) 16.45-48

"Whale Road, The" (Akers) 18.102-03

"Whalesong" (Tyrer) 17.75

"What Came of the Search" (Withrow) 15.29

"What If Atlantis . . . ?" (Reiter) 14.7

"When Cyber Things Return" (Gold) 17.107

"Where the New Gods Dwell" (Gold) 13.68-69

"Whippoorwill, The" (Lopez) 16.68-71

"Whisper to Rock, A" (Reed) 18.58-59

"Whispers from a Crematory Skull" (Pérez-Campos) 17.112-13

"Wicker King's Palace, The" (Gold) 14.24-25

"Widow, The" (Khoa) 14.32-36

"Wild Hunt, The" (Arrington) 12.58

"Wildfires" (Sng) 12.89-91

"Willing Sacrifice, A" (White) 19.72

"Witch in the House, A" (Smith) 12.45-47

"Witch of Hearts, The" (Arrington) 11.16-17

"Witch, The" (Kerestman) 19.60-61

"Witch-Gallows, The" (Maybrook) 13.62

"Witch's Cat, The" (Davitt) 12.85

"Witch's Tit" (Arenas) 15.89

"Witch's Tree, The" (Hardy) 17.38-39

"Witchbirds" (Lopez) 19.30-32

"Within the Wood" (Wildes) 15.80

"Word, A" (Reiter) 15.115

"Woses, The" (Coffman) 14.14-15

"Wraith of the Versifier" (Barker) 13.40

"Wretched Raft" (Boylan) 12.23

"Written in Smoke" (Schwader) 16.66

"Xipe Totec" (Davitt) 12.20-21

"Yethwood" (Smith) 17.72-74

"Zeohyr's Allure" (Couturier) 17.108-9

"Zombie Moon" (Curtis) 16.60-61

"Zwartenberg the Necromancer" (Arenas) 16.98-99

www.ingramcontent.com/pod-product-compliance
Lightning Source LLC
Chambersburg PA
CBHW060806050426
42449CB00008B/1559